BASICS

MATERIALS

\\MANFRED HEGGER \\HANS DREXLER
\\MARTIN ZEUMER

BASICS

MATERIALS

BIRKHÄUSER – PUBLISHERS FOR ARCHITECTURE
BASEL · BOSTON · BERLIN

CONTENTS

\\Foreword _7

\\Introduction _8

\\Principles for the choice of materials _11
 \\Perception of materials _12
 \\Material requirements _17
 \\Technical properties _24

\\Classification of materials _27
 \\Typologies of building materials _27
 \\Wood _33
 \\Timber-based products _36
 \\Natural stone _39
 \\Concrete _42
 \\Mineral-bonded masonry units _45
 \\Boards with mineral binders _48
 \\Plaster and screeds_51
 \\Ceramics and bricks _54
 \\Metals _57
 \\Glass _62
 \\Plastics _66
 \\Textiles and membranes _69

\\Designing with materials _73
 \\General conditions _73
 \\Basing design on material _75
 \\Materializing the design _76
 \\Design approaches _78

\\In conclusion _85

\\Appendix _86
 \\Literature _86
 \\Picture credits _87

FOREWORD

The materials out of which a building is made play a crucial part in its effect and impact. They are important not just as the basis for construction, but also as a mediator between building and people. Materials have a story to tell about the building, its structure and its function. Surfaces are perceived by the senses, and convey feelings. Materials can open a building up to the outside world, can seem light and transparent, and the building can also appear monolithic and solid – the choice of material is part of design, in order to make the desired impression in terms of architectural language. So the material qualities of a building must be chosen and used with care. They should support the design, and where applicable even help to shape it. The possibilities offered by different materials are many and varied, making them an ideal design resource for architects.

The "Basics" series works through the important principles of a new field of activity stage by stage, and provides a sound and useful instrument for studying architecture. It does not set out to be a comprehensive collection of specialist knowledge, but to give students readily comprehensible explanations and foster their understanding of the important issues and parameters in the various subject areas.

The "Materials" volume chooses to address the substantive properties of materials and building components first and foremost. The authors do not therefore provide a comprehensive survey, but concentrate on essential subject matter for design and the way the building is later perceived. The focus is on the insightful use of different materials and the wide range of design possibilities they offer. First, their key properties are identified, so that readers can find their way around the physical and emotional world of material. The book systematically introduces the most important building material types and characterizes their individual properties. Typical design approaches and principles in handing the material quality of buildings are also explained.

With the aid of the "Materials" volume, students will be able to acquire knowledge about using different materials, so that they can make their designs and ideas lively and expressive.

Bert Bielefeld
Editor

INTRODUCTION

Architecture lends material form to a design idea. Translating this idea into built reality and the effect it makes on viewers is essentially determined by the choice of material. An enormous variety of materials is available, but a good design is inevitably restricted to very specific material qualities.

But what does material quality mean? As is common in current architectural discussion, this is a borrowed term, liberally used, but ambiguous and imprecise. The term "material quality" is often applied to the surface of architecture. Materials contribute to the spatial experience by their appearance, how they feel when touched, their smell, and their acoustic characteristics.

By referring to visible material quality, we attempt to get round the reservation that the surface represents only part of material quality as a whole. But perception involves more human senses than just sight, which suggests that material quality must be more than the structure of a surface.

This point is clarified by a philosophical definition that coined the term material quality. It suggests that a body consists of matter – of a material substance – but also conveys a sense of physical presence. So material quality arises from the material, and in this definition, many aspects of materials fuse into a unity.

However, this explanation does not include all the topics included in the concept of material quality. As well as the surface, the internal structure and the resultant emergence of a physical entity, there is also an associative plane, which is particularly significant in architecture. Materials can be associated with and symbolize states of affairs. The fact that stone stands for wealth and power can be grasped in any banking quarter. Thus, there are three levels of meaning: visible, inner, and associative material quality.

Perceiving material quality is based on a personal, individual position, which is neither right nor wrong. Many distinguished architects have developed their own points of view, which they place in the context of material quality: Alvar Aalto, Tadao Ando, Louis Kahn, to name only a few, have used their choice of materials to put a lasting stamp on their architecture.

Effortless handling of materials and delight taken in experimenting with them enrich architecture. The attraction of the new plays a key part. Every architect is familiar with this. Many use choice of material as an innovative device to make their buildings unique. That choice offers possibilities that are increasingly becoming central themes in architecture.

Variety of material, and its alienation, exploring the limits of what is technically possible, deliberately misusing materials or transferring material from use areas unrelated to architecture are some of the stylistic devices used by today's architects.

Choosing material requires knowledge of a large number of hard facts. But it also needs intuition and a feeling for the suitable material in a particular architectural context. This book will first examine material quality in terms of objectively verifiable, "hard" factors. Important questions include: what external conditions are materials exposed to, and how do these affect them? How can the choice of material be systematized? Once this basis has been established, "soft" factors become central. The book will thus guide readers from the range of possibilities offered by materials via design strategies to possible positions that develop from material quality.

In the chapter "Principles for the choice of materials" the reader will be introduced to the basic issues relating to handling materials. It points out the central influences affecting the course of material life cycles, and provides the means for sensible evaluation. The chapter "Classification of materials" explains criteria for choice, capacities and fields of application for selected building materials. Specifications are given for possible performance based on the properties of materials, and brought together as a material use catalogue. Finally, the chapter "Designing with materials" discusses different ways of designing out of and with materials. The various design approaches or principles are described and explained to give the reader ideas and indicate the field of possibilities for handling materials, or how a design problem can be approached from this perspective.

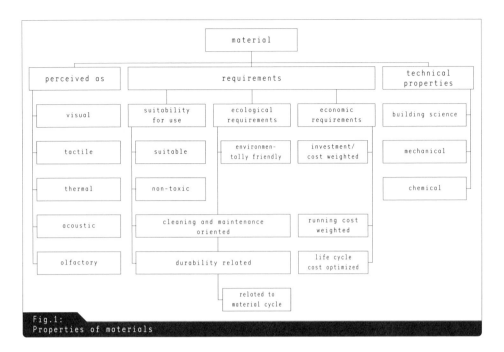

Fig.1:
Properties of materials

PRINCIPLES FOR THE CHOICE OF MATERIALS

For a long time, there was little choice of building materials. There were few materials available, but they were universally known. Knowledge about how to deal with them was developed and handed down over generations. The onset of industrialization gradually broke down this historically matured manageable quality. Today we have an immense number of materials at our disposal. Specialists such as "material scouts" provide architects with information about materials and innovations. The field of possible performance has also grown with the number of materials available.

\\ Hint:
The term "material scout" is not a precise description of a profession but is a possible area in which an architect can work, researching or developing new and innovative materials, systematizing knowledge about the use of building materials for special purposes, and supporting designing architects by providing creative ideas.

Architects are not expected to be familiar with all these properties in detail, but they should be aware of connections and consequences. They will combine all levels on which materials can be considered in a knowledge of their properties, within a design and in the later execution stages. The design process is driven by properties relating to perception, as well as ecological, economic and technical properties, and those related to use.
> Fig. 1

PERCEPTION OF MATERIALS

The effect made by materials is discerned by all the senses. The following come into play:

_ Visual sense – sight
_ Tactile sense – touch
_ Thermal sense – feeling
_ Auditory sense – hearing
_ Olfactory sense – smell

Visual

For humans, about 90 percent of information stimuli are based on the sense of sight. So it is hardly surprising that visual considerations are usually the first basis for making decisions about building materials.

Surface perception

Sight is based on transmitted rays. The corresponding material property is the reflection of rays from the surface of the material. The light striking a material therefore plays a key part in visual perception. The skin of the building materials, from glossy to matte, from light to dark, from homogeneous to textured, is the basis for architectural design. The neutral smoothness of industrially manufactured surfaces can be just as fascinating as sensitively controlled elements of roughness, which are sometimes perceptible only at second glance. Three-dimensional structures acquire greater depth if light strikes the texture at an acute angle. Careful placing of windows or light sources can enhance the three-dimensional quality of the materials. > Fig. 2

Transparency

This effect can be so greatly reinforced by transparent materials that it seems to work regardless of the material used. Semi-transparent, evenly textured planes, such as glass or plastic, can be superimposed; perforated opaque materials can also be used. The effect created – interference – changes the appearance of the building according to the angle from which it is viewed. The building is enlivened, and large even surfaces can acquire an enhanced sense of vivacity. > Fig 3

Colour

A building material's colour also has an important part to play. If the material is light in colour, it makes a particularly strong three-

Fig.2:
Texture of a concrete surface

Fig.3:
Interference caused by printing on glass

dimensional impact, as the eye registers the contrast – the difference in brightness – before the colour quality. This contrast is particularly great in light-coloured materials because of shadows cast. Dark materials offer very little contrast, and so their surfaces lose their plastic quality, and tend to look two-dimensional.

Colours influence the way space is perceived. Warm colours make a space look smaller, while cold ones make it look bigger. Colours can also affect users on a subconscious, emotional plane: cold colours are distancing, but warm colours are stimulating.

Scale

The size and scale of building materials and surfaces also help to determine the impression they make. Different textural dimensions influence perception from close up, and in the middle and far distance. A material's effect is thus defined by the degree of prefabrication, element size, texturing, jointing, and other surface treatments. In this way, the choice of materials can match a particular building to its surroundings or make it stand out from them. › Fig. 4

Association

The almost endless variety of visual stimuli is reduced to those that are important for viewers in the perception process, and made into a personal image through their own knowledge. The architect can take advantage of this by playing with familiar associations. For example, using unusual small brick formats on a façade can make a building seem particularly generous, as a result of subconscious assumptions about scale.
› Fig. 5

13

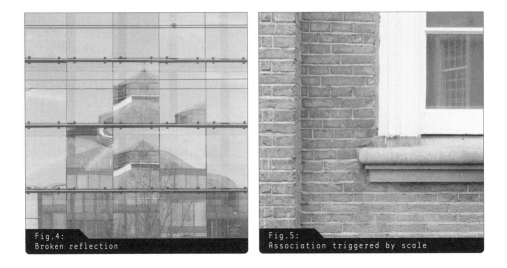

Fig.4:
Broken reflection

Fig.5:
Association triggered by scale

Tactile

In tactile perception, the whole body becomes a sense organ, and particularly the hands. They explore the contact areas of the materials and their properties: even or rough, smooth or dull, hard or soft, cold or warm. > Fig. 6

Handles and handrails offer a particular good hold if the hand can grasp them completely. Soft materials yield to the hand, and can thus make a handle seem particularly pleasant. Construction elements that seem warm invite touch, and encourage people to use features like parapets and window-seats. > Fig. 7

Surface temperatures, radiation and reflection in construction elements influence thermal sensations via the skin. There is a pleasant and apparently warm impression if the components that are touched draw little heat out of the body, as in materials with a low thermal mass and high radiation. Heavy building materials, such as steel and concrete, draw heat out of the body when touched and thus seem cold.

Thermal

This principle also works without contact, as people register the temperature difference between the air and adjacent surfaces. Lack of radiation is interpreted as cold. In contrast, solid surfaces exposed to the sun can, later, at night, seem to be warm.

A total of four factors play a crucial part in human thermal perception: the speed at which air is moving, air temperature, radiation from

Fig.6:
Rough, hard and cold handrail

Fig.7:
Door handle wrapped in leather

› ⋒

Indoor climate

adjacent surfaces, and air humidity. These factors combine to create the climate within a space. Humidity particularly affects thermal comfort. If it rises, the perceived temperature rises as well. Materials with sorptive properties can regulate humidity. Such materials, particularly plaster and clay, but also other solid building materials, can contribute to a particularly pleasant indoor climate. › Fig. 8

Materials with a low thermal mass can thus create a "shack climate", which is strongly affected by temperatures brought into the building from the outside – especially when it is extremely hot or cold. The reverse is the "castle climate": heavy building materials with a high thermal mass help to create a stable climate by reducing temperature amplitude, decoupling the space from extreme exterior temperatures.

⋒
\\ Hint:
Sorption enables a building material to draw moisture out of the air and store it on its surface. Moisture is absorbed or released in relation to humidity.

Fig.8:
Clay thermal wall

Senses working together

With sight taking the lead, other sensory experiences help to concretize material qualities. Hearing and smell are important, as well as the senses that have already been mentioned. For example, the muted crunch made by the round grains of sand can be heard when walking along a sandy path. The smell of wood is associated with wellbeing. The more senses a material addresses, the sooner a satisfying overall experience can be created by a material or a space.

Designers have two possible ways of deliberately stimulating and enhancing perception: one is to present the channels of perception with contrasting experiences, for example through an unexpected tactile effect contrasting with the visual one. The anticipated sensation is missing, and this sense of disturbance becomes an experience. But it can also produce a subconscious feeling of discomfort if inconsistencies of this kind go beyond a certain level.

Conversely, materials can create a particularly all-embracing and harmonious overall image. Agreements, harmony between the visual impression and the other levels of perception create physical wellbeing. The individual impressions complement each other, and combine to form a satisfying overall image. Architecture then achieves its aim through a wide range of perceptions open to simultaneous experience. But this image can tip over as well, in the direction of emotional overload and ultimately banality.

Contrast

Agreement

MATERIAL REQUIREMENTS

Every material must fulfil its function in terms of specific requirements. Its use-related properties determine the utility value of a property
for its owners and users, so they address this purpose directly. The demands placed on materials can be broken down into four groups:

_ Comfort requirements
_ Protection from effects of the environment
_ Maintaining function
_ Low environmental pollution

Comfort requirements

Materials meet comfort requirements at the points where their surfaces come into direct contact with the user. Such points include floor,
wall and ceiling surfaces in particular, or movable parts such as doors and
windows. Comfort can be expressed in technical values to only a limited
extent. Very few specifications for individual properties can be quantified,
> see chapter Technical properties such as the antistatic performance of elastic
floor coverings. In other areas designers are left to their own experience
and feelings.

Safe for health

> 🔖

Comfortable
temperature

One fundamental demand made on any material is that it should not
be a risk to human health, and consequently hygiene. Harmful materials
are often suspected as such long before it can be proved.

Materials that are concealed within the structure often contribute
to a feeling of atmospheric and climatic comfort within a building. Heat-
insulating materials prevent the building from losing energy, and ensure
that surface and air temperatures do not fall below a pleasant level. Thermal mass enables materials to match surface and air temperature, capture
moisture from the air and thus smooth out the temperature and humidity
within a space. Wind seals, draughtproof layers in wall superstructures,
reduce air movement that can cause discomfort, as do seals on moving elements such as doors and windows.

🔖

\\ Hint:
Memory is also linked with sensory perception,
so stimulating many senses makes memories more
likely to last.

🔖

\\ Hint:
Substances posing an element of risk are most
often found in surface coatings, adhesives and
binders, but also in elastic or textile coverings. Careful research is recommended.

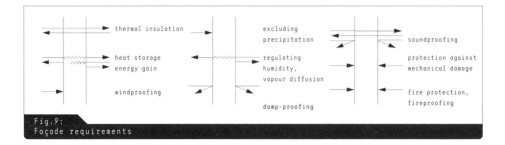

Fig.9:
Façade requirements

Acoustic comfort is achieved by eliminating disturbing sound emissions. Airborne sound can be kept to a minimum by building materials with open-pored surfaces. Correctly dimensioned, sound-absorbing surfaces – elastic and fine-pored materials – reduce echo in rooms and make speech more readily understood. Building materials reduce the transmission of structure-borne sound by their mass. If a particular part of a building cannot be solid, different layer thicknesses and uncoupled structures may help to keep resonance down in light constructions.

Protection from effects of the environment

Buildings are required to offer protection, from environmental influences in particular. As the interface between inside and outside, façades have to meet a wide range of conditions, which also relate to the use of the building. › Fig. 9

Airborne chemical substances (such as free radicals, or ozone) attack the structure of the material. This can lead to surface changes that increase susceptibility to dirt, or reduce transparency or translucency. Only UV-resistant materials should therefore be used for cladding the building.

\\ Hint:
We distinguish between noise and sound. Noise usually has negative connotations. Sounds are characteristic of certain things and situations. The information they convey makes a positive contribution to wellbeing, independently of volume.

Materials exposed to weather or used in damp areas must be damp-proof. Functional elements that carry the water-bearing layer over material edges and joints can help to emphasize material quality. Frost protection is linked with this. The penetration of damp, which increases in volume when it freezes, causes tensions within the material and can ultimately destroy it. Particular attention should be paid to water that exerts pressure or rises from the ground, as it is extremely difficult to optimize material performance subsequently in such cases. For example, masonry walls should be protected against rising damp by a horizontal damp course.

Thermal expansion is also important. According to temperature, materials expand (warm) or contract (cold). If there is insufficient space for longitudinal expansion, forces will build up. If two materials with differing degrees of hardness are adjacent at such points, the softer one will inevitably be damaged. The distances between the individual construction elements should therefore be great enough for them not to touch each other – thus creating gaps. The necessary pattern of gaps can emerge from design, construction or regulations. The size of the gap itself derives from the length and longitudinal expansion of the selected material.

Maintaining function

Materials have to fulfil their functions in daily use, not just under laboratory conditions. This includes improper use. If the edges of a material are insufficiently durable, edges, corner reinforcements can both assist structurally and draw attention to particular material properties as a design feature.

Hardness, abrasion resistance and load classes define a material's resistance to friction. Floors, in particular, have to meet heavy demands: increased abrasion leads from decreased lustre to heavy wear on the surface of the material. Performance can be correspondingly enhanced by measures like clean walking areas, with large shoe scrapers at the entrances to buildings. These can have a material quality of their own; they can be

🔲

\\ Hint:
Hardness is the material property that resists abrasion. Abrasion is wear to a material at a precisely defined load, while load classes categorize materials according to comparable wear behaviour.

Fig.10:
Recycled brick wall with extension

Fig.11:
Ageing in a timber façade

made of metal, plastic or textiles, and may also match the floor covering that follows.

Maintenance
needed

The need for surfaces that need little care and maintenance should be considered even at the design stage. Cleaning represents a particular kind of demand in its own right, as it can also cause abrasion or lasting damage to surfaces. Skirting boards protect walls from being damaged by cleaning at the point where they meet the floor. Details of this kind, which seem unimportant at first, are actually omnipresent, and help to make architecture more expressive in terms of its materials.

Durability

Materials should be able to perform for as long and as often as possible. This attribute is defined technically as durability. If a building has a finite useful life, as in exhibition centres, for example, the degree of durability can be planned appropriately in advance. If it cannot, all materials should be as durable as possible. Each material has its own useful life, according to functional demands. It should therefore be possible to replace

\\ Hint:
Durability, or useful life, defines the period for which a building element can remain usable.

20

Fig.12:
Graffiti in the Reichstag

Fig.13:
Ageless glass façade

any functional component without destroying another. This requirement raises the subject of layered structures, in walls for example, which contain technical equipment, protective surfaces, insulating materials and loadbearing structures. › Fig. 10

Ageing

Ageing processes are evidence of transience and decay; expressed positively, they illustrate temporal qualities and life. Just like people, buildings and their materials can age with dignity. After a certain time, almost any material shows traces of the wear and tear it has undergone, whether from external influences or from use. This ageing can take the form of a natural patina, which may be very attractive, and so can be caused deliberately. An oxide layer creates a patina on metal, on weatherproof steel, for example, or on bronze.

Ageing is clearly demonstrated by larch as a façade cladding: the material first turns grey from its original reddish hue as a response to weathering, through the effects of UV radiation. The radiation breaks down the natural colour pigments in the wood, although they survive longer in protected areas. › Fig. 11 Materials considered particularly innovative at first can decline in aesthetic appeal as they age rapidly, and the signs of ageing show. They then quickly cease looking up-to-date.

If ageing processes and traces of use are accepted, these also model the material. Retaining such traces can tell a story of the distant past. › Fig. 12

Some materials, such as glass or polished stone, show no visible signs of ageing. Time seems to pass them by without trace. › Fig. 13.

Environmental pollution

Building uses a very high proportion of resources and creates the most waste. Decisions made during the planning process thus have considerable environmental consequences. Over the life cycle of a building, high ecological impacts go hand in hand with additional expenditure. For this reason too, it makes considerable sense to look more closely at environmental pollution when choosing materials.

Entropy

For example, using aluminium consumes a great deal of energy and water for the treatment of the bauxite. This means there is more heavy metal in the water and ultimately the food cycle. This triggers a process of substance flows known as entropy. The aim should always be to minimize substance flows in order to keep entropy down.

› 🛈
Material cycle

The ideal way of using material is within a closed substance circle: refuse can become a secondary raw material. The quality of recycling is crucial to its ecological value, to retaining the parent substance and the energy stored in the material. We distinguish between reuse (repeated use of the material), alternate use (recovering basic chemicals from refuse) and extended use (using treated refuse for new purposes). There is also a distinction between downcycling (material loop with declining material quality) and recycling (material loop with the same material quality).

Life-cycle
assessment

Life cycle assessments are a comprehensive method of evaluating building materials from the point of view of environmental technology. Various harmful materials are weighted within impact categories so that they can be allotted a characteristic value, with the unit identifying the most important harmful substance. Key impact categories are primary energy content, greenhouse effect and ozone depletion potential. › Tab. 1

🛈

\\ Hint:
Entropy identifies the mixture of substance
and energy flows, effectively the increase
of disorder in the world. In a closed system
(such as the earth), it can never be reduced,
but always thrusts towards a maximum.

Independently of the choice of materials, it is generally the case that:

_ reduction to structural essentials can be advantageous.
_ durable, light structures are generally preferable to massive ones.
_ the use of materials that retain CO_2 is a positive factor.
_ invisible building components are particularly suitable for problem-free optimization.
_ the longer a building is intended to be used, the more important it is to consider this phase of use.
_ building components with short useful lives are more environmentally polluting because renewal costs accumulate more rapidly.
_ in housing construction, the environmental impact made by building materials is particularly significant, because they are generally used in small pieces, and the level of finish is high.

The ecological criteria of a building material are increasingly becoming a factor. They do not hinder the planning process, but in fact enrich it, and can generate additional creativity by asking new questions and posing alternatives. For example, if materials are reused in prominent positions › Fig. 10 they can be seen as evidence of a sustainable approach, and then create an additional plane of significance for building materials.

Tab.1:
Selected impact categories in a life cycle assessment

Characteristic values of a life cycle assessment in building	Abbreviation	Unit
Primary energy content (non-renewable)	PEI	MJ
Primary energy content (renewable)	PEI	MJ
Greenhouse potential	GWP 100	kg CO_2 eq
Ozone depletion potential	ODP	kg CCL_3F eq
Acidification potential	AP	kg SO_2 eq
Eutrophication potential	EP	kg PO_4^{3-} eq
Photo-oxidant formation ("summer smog potential")	POCP	kg C_2H_4 eq

TECHNICAL PROPERTIES

Technical properties are key criteria in material selection. A particular material can be chosen only by considering its technical performance, in other words on the basis of its "inner values", its physical, mechanical and chemical parameters.

Physical
properties

Basic physical specifications are available for all building materials: gross density is a core value that enables other properties such as thermal mass or thermal conductivity capacity to be deduced, thus giving an initial overall technical impression of a material.

Mechanical
properties

Mechanical properties place particular constraints on the potential use of a material for construction. They include the material's strength and rigidity, its response to forces acting on it through plastic or elastic distortion, and its surface hardness. Mechanical properties are linked in many ways with thermodynamic properties and those relating to moisture, e.g. the frost resistance of natural stone. One important mechanical characteristic of natural stone is its abrasion resistance, the extent to which it can resist mechanical friction. This correlates with high density and high compressive strength, again the basis for a low water absorption coefficient. This is a key feature for frost resistance, and is determined by a stone's porosity and capillarity. A high value, as for sandstone, for example, means that the stone has to be protected from water penetrating. The most important characteristics are summarized in Table 2. › Tab. 2

Chemical
properties

The chemical behaviour of a building material can change through direct contact with chemicals or environmental influences. They include corrosion (especially of metals), leaching of salts (in mineral-bound materials, ceramics), resistance to UV light (materials including plastics), and reactions to other building materials (for adhesives, mastics etc.).

Questions
in choosing
material

The key questions when selecting a material arise mainly from the intended effect and the requirements profile:

\\Hint:
The Mohs hardness scale places materials in relation to each other by creating groups of materials that will scratch the next softer one. The scale ranges from 1 (talc) to 10 (diamond).

\\Hint:
The vapour diffusion resistance value identifies how much greater the resistance to water vapour is compared to an air layer of identical thickness.

Properties	Characteristic	Symbol	Unit
Physical properties	Gross density	ρ	kg/m³
	Thermal conductivity	λ	W/mK
	Specific thermal capacity	c	J/kgK
	Thermal storage number	S	–
Mechanical properties	Mohs scale hardness	HM	Wh/m²K
	Compressive strength	f_c	N/mm²
	Tensile strength	f_t	N/mm²
	Modulus of elasticity	E	N/mm²
Thermodynamic properties	Thermal expansion coefficient	α	1/K
Moisture-related	Vapour diffusion resistance value	m	–
	Water absorption coefficient	ω	kg/m²h$^{0.5}$

Tab.2:
Important properties with units

_ Which human sense should be stimulated, and how will people perceive the material?
_ What natural and use-related influences will the intended function have on the material?

These questions can be answered in terms of specific material qualities, which can usually be reduced a few technical properties. Conversely, the properties of a material can give rise to a wide variety of new and innovative possible uses and applications, some of them surprising.

CLASSIFICATION OF MATERIALS

The properties of certain selected building materials are set out in greater detail below. Once the key characteristics of a material have been established for a particular purpose, it becomes possible to compare materials with each other. The first step is to divide materials into groups with similar property profiles. This considerably reduces the difficulty of making comparisons, and sharpens the designer's eye for the performance to be expected from a group of materials, or a specific material.

TYPOLOGIES OF BUILDING MATERIALS

If alternatives are being sought for materials, it makes sense to structure the initially overwhelming variety of materials and characteristics according to type. Materials are distinguished by their composition, structure and the way they are manufactured. This speeds up the selection process and can promote the discovery of interesting alternatives.

Typology based on material composition
Under material composition we first distinguish organic and inorganic materials. › Tab. 3

Mineral building materials are always first associated with solid building components, and metal components with flat components or those in the form of bars, because of their high performance.

Non-homogeneous building materials
However, these associations work only for homogeneous building materials. If compound materials are used, individual components often

Tab.3:
Building materials classified according to material composition

| | Inorganic materials | | Organic materials |
	Mineral	Metallic	
Selected materials	Natural stone	Metals	Wood
	Concrete		Bitumen
	Glass		Plastics
	Brick		
Dependent properties			
- Density	Average	High	Low
- Strength	Brittle, high compressive strength, low tensile strength	Tough, high compressive and tensile strength	Tough, dependent on internal structure
- Thermal conductivity	Average	High	Low
- Combustibility	Not combustible	Not combustible	Largely combustible

> Q

cover different functions within a structural element. A concrete floor is a
good illustration here: although its surface suggests a homogeneous stone
material, the structural steel it contains absorbs tensile forces. Structural
sections consisting of various components are affected by a complex interplay of the individual components' properties and quantities. For example,
the specific pH of the concrete prevents the steel from corroding. The steel
in turn prevents the concrete floor from sagging, thus avoiding the forma-
tion of cracks. So it is only when the materials start to work together that
the just use of materials is fully in evidence, with every single material
making the maximum contribution to the whole.

This philosophy for optimizing properties systematically is increasingly being practised. For example, glass has for some time not been a
single material but a whole group of materials with a wide range of available properties, surface treatments and layering sequences, which opens
up endless possibilities of function and design. Remarkable and innovative architectural achievements are now usually based on the interplay
between materials and familiar surfaces.

Tab.4:
Structural classification of building materials

	Amorphous material	Crystalline materials	Fibrous materials
Selected materials	Glass	Metals	Wood
	Plastics	Clay	
	Bitumen	Brick	
Dependent properties			
– Direction	Non-directional	Largely non-directional	Directional
– Thermal conductivity	Lower than for crystalline materials	Higher than for amorphous materials	Low
– Strength	Tougher than crystalline materials	More brittle than amorphous materials	High tensile strength in the grain direction

Fig.14:
Wooden loadbearing structure

Fig.15:
Various wood products

Typology based
on structural
composition

Another way of classifying materials is their structural composition.
› Tab. 4

The structure of fibrous elements such as wood can make a striking contribution to the design. For example, they can form a loadbearing level, or a complex loadbearing system by bending. › Fig. 14

Typology based
on production

Another way of classifying materials is based on how they are obtained or produced, the first subdivision being into natural and artificial materials. On a second level, a distinction can be made between amorphous, intermediate and shaped materials, and semi-finished products. The way in which a material is obtained is also a factor: natural materials are always produced by subtractive processes, while additive processes and those concerned only with shaping can be applied to artificial materials. › Tab. 5

Tab.5:
Materials classified according to production

	Natural materials	Artificial materials
Obtained by	Extraction process	Production of parent substances
Production	Raw material Processed material	Amorphous materials Intermediate materials Shaped materials
Process	Subtractive	Subtractive Additive Shaping

29

Finally, building materials differ from each other in their dimensions. Filler materials have low dependency levels and need a structural envelope. Small-format materials need to be combined if they are to form an effective structural element. This is achieved by further processing based on the dimensions of each material. Repetition and jointing create their own aesthetic. In contrast, large-format materials can be a structural element, e.g. a shear wall. They have to take up aspects of the building grid and the façade design on the level of construction and function.

Classifying materials typologically can provide information about how they are used, the extent to which they can be worked, and their architectural potential. Thus, for natural materials, the existing dimensions can be the essential criterion for use, or the way they are obtained can deliberately be left showing in the resultant material. › Fig. 15

The more elaborately a natural material is processed, the more its natural appearance is lost. The effects of the manufacturing process and subsequent work stand out more clearly, and the natural variations in the material shift into the background. The use of industrial production in architecture can go so far as to explore the constantly changing technical boundaries of a process in a completely new way. › Fig. 16

In this way, every material and its performance characteristics contribute to the way space is designed. The diversity of materials and ways in which they can be deployed opens up almost inexhaustible possibilities for giving architecture a quite specific material quality and impact, appealing to all the human senses. Examples of these possibilities and potentials are assessed below for the most important building materials, and also compared with each other in terms of material specifications.

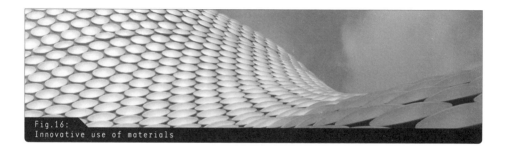

Fig.16:
Innovative use of materials

Material	Properties	Use
Wood (see page 33)	Natural directional building material, easy to work; high tensile and compressive strength in grain direction; moisture-dependent expansion; low weight and thermal conductivity; natural, strong, rough texture in conifers and oak, fine texture in maple, beech and birch.	The directional structure is suitable for loadbearing structures and loadbearing layers, which can also provide thermal insulation; façade cladding through accumulations and overlapping of boards and shingles; high-quality furniture and handles.
Timber products (see page 36)	Made of wood, and share its properties; the directional structure is reorganized as required when producing panels; reasonably priced production from timber waste	Directional panels or beams are used for loadbearing structures or reinforcement; non-directional timber products are used for furniture, built-in units, cladding and insulation.
Natural stone (see page 39)	Natural inorganic building material with a stratified or homogenous structure according to origin; high density, hardness, compressive strength, thermal conductivity and storage capacity, and resistance to weathering; elaborate extraction and processing, creating special material effects.	The compressive strength of stone is exploited for loadbearing masonry; slabs are sufficient for using most of the properties; this produces a surface design supported by a substructure, as a façade or floor covering.
Concrete (see page 42)	As liquid stone, shares similar properties with natural stone; properties can be changed by additives; concrete loses volume when worked and needs a secondary loadbearing system.	Pressure-loaded shell loadbearing structures; can absorb tensile forces only in combination with steel or other materials: it is then suitable for freely shaped construction elements and loadbearing structures.
Prefabricated mineral units (see page 45)	Properties similar to natural stone; gross density and thermal conductivity are usually lower; shrinks little in production, which means high dimensional stability.	Masonry with a low proportion of joints for a monolithic effect; possible single-shell use in cases of low thermal conductivity; can also be used in sheet form for floor coverings.
Mineral slabs (see page 48)	Have similar properties to prefabricated mineral units; usually non-homogeneous structure (e.g. reinforcement or packaging) as a material compound for increased strength and lower weight.	Cladding for walls and upright structures, cement-bound also as façade cladding; functional materials for sound- and fireproofing.
Screeds / rendering (see page 51)	According to binding agent, high strength, seal tightness and surface hardness, or low strength, damp inhibiting and vapour permeable; similar properties to prefabricated mineral units; elasticity provided by additives.	Functional protective layers for frost-, damp- and fireproofing; screeds as pressure-distributing floor slabs; rendering as wall and ceiling cladding with multiple textures.

Materials	Properties	Use
Ceramics / bricks (see page 54)	Inorganic material with high strength, hardness and thermal conductivity, which can be reduced by additives and shaping; high capillarity of earthenware, low for sintered ware; high production-related dimensional tolerances.	Bricks are used for masonry based on the octametric system, also in single-shell form in cases of low thermal conductivity; can be used in sheet form for façade cladding and floor coverings.
Metals (see page 57)	Shiny elastic material with high density and resistance to compressive and tensile forces; high thermal and electrical conductivity; corrosion, which forms a durable protective coating on some metals; wide variety of possible shapes.	Statically optimized bars for load-bearing structures or concrete reinforcement; thin sheets and panels for cladding, especially for exterior use; prefabricated parts, e.g. bearings, handles, pipework.
Glass (see page 62)	Amorphous, brittle and transparent material with a high gross density, compressive strength and hardness; load-bearing capacity dependent on surface tension; average thermal conductivity, reduced in combination with coatings.	Transparent façades and windows; wide variety of surface finishes can reduce light permeability or admit light on one side only if a reflective surface is applied.
Plastics (see page 66)	Usually translucent, dense organic material with low thermal conductivity and gross density; elasticity, high tensile strength and temperature expansion; almost any property can be generated by compound or composition.	Universally useful material, from high-strength fibre-compound sections via interior finish and façade panels to sealing strips or membranes; functional materials e.g. coatings or adhesives.
Textiles and membranes (see page 69)	Soft materials with low thermal conductivity, suitable only for tensile loads; two-dimensional structure, three-dimensional only with felting; waterproof with coating.	Suitable for weatherproofing as a stretched material; home floor and wall coverings, mobile room dividers, coverings for seating and handles; felt for acoustic separation of components.

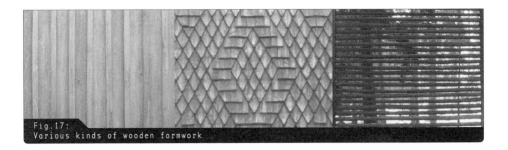

Fig.17:
Various kinds of wooden formwork

WOOD

Wood is almost universally available as a renewable building material. It can be used in a variety of ways and is reasonably priced. It is easy to work, and has an individual smell according to species. Wooden surfaces have natural colour and texture, and can become darker or lighter. Wood draws little heat out of the human body when touched, and so is experienced as pleasant, sensual and warm.

Structure and properties

Because of its cellular structure, wood has a fibrous or grainy structure, is low in weight and high in strength. As the fibres lie longitudinally within the trunk, it can absorb greater tensile, pressure and bending loads in this direction than laterally to the grain. It is thus best to load wood in the same way as the tree itself was loaded by weight and wind loads. › Fig. 18 At the same time it has low thermal conductivity combined with high heat storage capacity. Wood also has a high CO_2 storage capacity, and is excellent in terms of return to the material cycle.

Swelling and shrinking

As well as expanding when the temperature rises, wood is also subject to moisture-dependent swelling and shrinkage. Wood stores water in its cells when humidity levels are high, and releases it again when humidity is low. This behaviour must be accommodated in planning and processing. Shrinkage cracks can occur when wood is dried, but they have little effect on static loadbearing properties. › Fig. 18

\\ Hint:
Wood has an organic composition very similar to plastic (see p. 66), a fibrous structure or grain, which is exploited when making wooden panels (see p. 36); it can be used very similarly to metal for construction purposes (see p. 57).

\\Important:
Many types of wood are particularly resistant to pests because they contain resin and other natural substances, and are thus very well suited for outdoor use; these include the Central European timber species oak and larch.

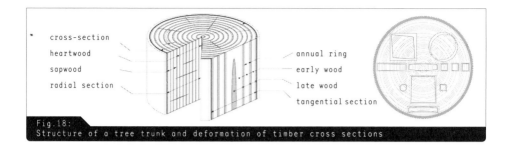

cross-section	annual ring
heartwood	early wood
sapwood	late wood
radial section	tangential section

Fig.18:
Structure of a tree trunk and deformation of timber cross sections

Timber species   The properties of wood vary considerably according to the species of tree, but they also depend on growth factors, which show in branch positioning and the annual rings in the wood. The fundamental classification is as coniferous or deciduous timber. Conifers, the older group in terms of evolution history, have a simpler cell-type structure and share very similar properties (e.g. gross density). Coniferous trees (spruce, pine, fir) grow more quickly, usually have strongly marked annual rings, and are less suitable for compressive and tensile loading. Deciduous timber is more specialized in its cell structure, depending on the species. Native deciduous species (oak, beech, maple) are denser and stronger than coniferous timbers. Deciduous trees can produces heartwood of a different colour, consisting of dead cells with deposited tanning agents. They offer a great variety of textures and colours, linked with various technical properties and possible uses.

Timber
protection

> 💡

    Wood is very durable if used correctly. When used outdoors it is vulnerable to weathering, pests and rot. The tanning agents in deciduous timber or resins in coniferous timber can provide natural protection. Structural timber protection means restricting the environmental effects in order to make the timber more durable. For façades this can be achieved with projecting roofs, structural protection for the timber's particularly absorbent outer surfaces, protection from splashing, and draining any moisture that may appear by means of dripping from the edges. For chemical timber protection, pest-inhibiting substances are painted onto the surface, impregnations forced into the fibres under pressure, or the timber can be heat-treated.

Solid wood for
construction

    The timber industry addresses the heterogeneity of this natural building material by classifying the wood by quality. Gluing wood produces laminated timber in which any growth damage to the individual timber parts can be eliminated.

    The long tradition of timber construction has led to a large number of building methods and timber structures. If wood is used for loadbearing structures, the dimensions of the timber products, mostly in strip, slat or plank form, suggest a skeleton construction method (e.g. truss and timber frame methods). But flat and solid methods using planks or logs can also be chosen; these also exploit the timber's good thermal insulation and heat retention properties. › Fig. 19

Boards and shingles

Boards and shingles can be fitted together to form flat areas in scale patterns, by overlapping or using tongue-and-groove details; outdoors as roof or façade cladding. Timber shingles are fitted in several layers, and are extremely durable. › Fig. 17 left / centre Boards or shingles can be used rough-sawn, planed or sanded. Structures intended as non-slip surfaces outdoors have a contoured timber surface. If parquet is used, textures or even pictures can be created by laying the units in different directions. Similarly to wooden louvres, these give different colour effects as light is refracted at different angles according to its incidence, thus contributing to the lively quality of a room. › Fig. 17 right

Veneers

Timber makes a particular impact on people, and not just through solid construction. Thin surface veneers applied to reasonably priced wood-based products have a similar effect. This means that rare and high-quality wood can be used in a variety of ways; particular textures can be achieved by the way it is cut. › Fig. 19 Sawn and sliced veneers produce a particularly high-quality surface, highlighting the knots and grain. Peeled veneers are available in an endless band of veneer, and can be used both for making hardwearing timber-based products and as decorative veneer. But if the veneer is to be visible, only timber species with a low-key texture such as birch, ash or maple are used, as otherwise unnatural grain patterns can emerge.

Fig.19:
Stacked wooden construction

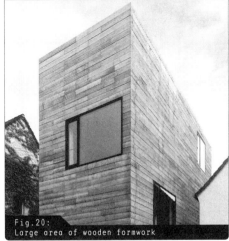

Fig.20:
Large area of wooden formwork

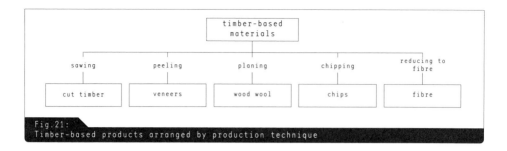

Fig.21:
Timber-based products arranged by production technique

TIMBER-BASED PRODUCTS

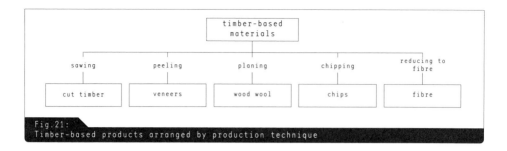 Wood or wood scraps are cut up or reduced in size to make timber-based products, and reassembled with or without a binder to produce a

new material. › Fig. 21

The fibrous structure of the timber is reorganized. This makes it possible to produce flat materials in stable shapes and with defined properties that can be manufactured industrially and are easy to work. They can either appear similar to natural wood, or create an alienating effect.

Timber-based products can be subdivided into veneer, chip and fibre products. › Fig. 22

Production and properties

Here, the natural properties of the wood shift into the background, although they are more or less retained visually according to the product concerned. Their strength derives from the pressure used in manufacture, and the strength of the timber component and the hardened binding agent. The position of the timber components in relation to each other defines the possible uses. The more directional the structure created is, the better suited the product is for structural items with a loadbearing requirement. The gross density increases in proportion to increasing strength (up to 1200 kg/m^3). The smaller the wood elements are, the more non-directional the overall structure becomes: a stratified sheet made up of flat veneer

\\ Hint:
Timber-based products are organic in composition, fibrous in structure, and similar to mineral-bonded panels in production and use (see page 48).

\\ Hint:
Bonding agents are responsible for the vapour emitted in timber-based product manufacture. These agents may contain toxic substances (see chapter Material requirements, Safe for health).

Fig.22:
Surface and cut end of veneered building plywood, chipboard and fibreboard

layers has a structure running on two axes because the individual layers are turned at right angles to each other, while a sheet of fibreboard is non-directional except for the sheet plane. Good insulation properties can be exploited as well as strength. The lowest gross density for fibreboard sheets lies at about 50 kg/m^3.

Surfaces

In contrast with wood, the surface and the internal structure of timber-based products differ. Higher-quality surface layers are chosen for veneered products, and these help to produce an even and more solid visual effect, and for chipboard products smaller chip material is used for the surface, which is more highly compressed in order to create an even surface for lamination. These differences in surface and internal structure can be seen at the cut ends of the timber-based products.

Lamination

Timber-based products also serve as reasonably prices support materials for high-quality veneers or other surfaces, especially on a plastic base. The borders between valuable natural wood veneers and imitations of natural wood (e.g. laminated floors) are becoming increasingly fluid. Like wood itself, timber-based products swell and shrink according to their moisture content, i.e. "move", so lamination on one side would produce tensions within the material, and later cause damage to the product or the surface. The appropriate surface is thus never applied to one side of the product only, but always to both sides. Every tension that arises is balanced by a counter-tension.

Possible uses

Timber-based products are used in fields ranging from structural engineering via cladding to built-in units and designer objects, and can be used indoors and out. When used in façades, structural timber protection acquires particular significance for the durability of the material in terms of weatherproofing, for example, or as a drip edge.

Structural uses

The great strength of the material is a key factor for structural use. Here, considerable creative potential is offered by its statical load rating associated with formability in relation to forces acting on it.

The limited dimensions of the sheets means that they require joints to be used for cladding. They may be joined with tongue and groove, the sheets can be overlapped, or a simple vertical joint can be used. The fact that timber-based products swell and shrink must be taken into account. The familiar creaking inside a building that is so typical of wood is caused by faulty jointing: tensions arising from shrinkage and temperature extension are being "discharged".

The fixing devices (screws, nails, clips) for timber-based products also present an opportunity for detailed surface design. Their material quality plays a key part in the architectural effect. They can be placed to be invisible, sunken and seen as part of the surface as a whole, or to draw attention as a second plane by the use of special underscrews with washers as pressure distributing elements.

In the case of built-in units, there is an interplay between the structural themes of material and surface performance. The diverse possibilities of timber-based products means that construction components can be shaped according to their utility value. It is possible to bend them on two or three axes by means of a special "baking" process. The flexibility of the products can be brought out here, as well as their strength.

> Fig. 23

Timber-based products are part of the timber cycle, and like it they store CO_2. Industrial manufacturing processes reduce the positive effect by 25 to 65 percent. Because the binder remains attached they are difficult to reprocess and are therefore usually incinerated to produce energy.

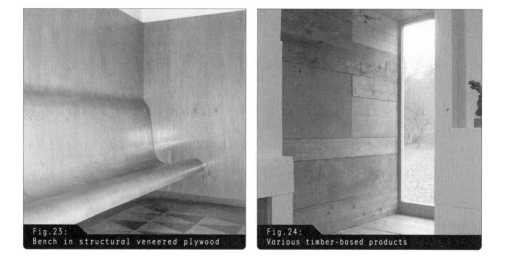

Fig.23:
Bench in structural veneered plywood

Fig.24:
Various timber-based products

Fig.25:
Igneous (granite), sedimentary (sandstone) and metamorphic stone (slate)

NATURAL STONE

> 🗍

Stability, authority and tradition are all associated with natural stone. It has a high gross density, great strength, great surface hardness and high thermal conductivity. Most stone resists natural processes such as weathering, frost and chemical processes, and is very durable. Despite, or precisely because of, these properties, natural stone has largely lost its statical function in modern architecture in favour of thin claddings as material for floor or façades. > Fig. 27

Availability

Natural stone is readily available, and stone typical of the region is used in many places. In this age of globalization, such local traditions are shifting into the background in favour of functional, aesthetic or financial considerations, as transport is also possible.

> 🗍

Petrographic
classification

The wide variety of natural stone types and terminology is impressive. Petrographic (stone science) and trade designations differ, but only the former are helpful for architects, as they bring natural stone types with similar properties together for comparison. Trade names can in fact be confusing; for example, "Belgian granite" is a type of limestone.

Natural stone falls into three groups: igneous, sedimentary and metamorphic. Igneous rocks are formed directly from liquid magma by cooling. They are particularly strong, hard and largely homogenous in structure. Sedimentary rocks are formed from particles. They can contain

🗍
\\ Hint:
Natural stones consist of inorganic material, vary in their structure and are similar to bricks in the way they are finished (see page 54) and prefabricated units with mineral binding agents. (see page 45).

🗍
\\ Hint:
Protecting resources in the case of natural stone is based on the key factors of landscape wear and tear, quarrying type, waste produced, and transport distance (see chapter Material requirements, Environmental pollution).

Fig.26:
Surface finishes for natural stone: pointed, bush-hammered, comb-chiselled, polished

a number of cavities, horizontal layers or even animal or vegetable fossils, according to the way in which they were formed. They are less strong than igneous rocks, but easier to work. Metamorphic rocks emerge from existing rock whose structure is changed by pressure, high temperatures or chemical processes. They are usually cavity-free, and have a distinctive texture. › Fig. 25

Granite

Granite (an igneous rock) is considered the most hardwearing natural stone used in the building industry, and it can be used almost without restrictions. It is strong, frost-resistant, largely resistant to weathering, and is available in a wide range of colours. Granite can be finished in any way required.

Sandstone

Sandstone (a sedimentary rock) is not as strong as granite and cannot be polished. It can absorb a great deal of water, so has only limited frost-resistance, and is susceptible to airborne pollution, and so weather-resistant to only a limited extent. It is considered very easy to work, however. Sandstone often has a slightly banded, open texture and is available in many colours.

Limestone

Limestone (a sedimentary rock) is the largest rock category used in the building industry. Its composition makes it susceptible to chemical processes. Limestone occurs in pastel shades, often contains fossils, and some of its varieties can be polished. Many types of limestone, including marble, are transparent when cut very thin.

Clay shale

Clay shale, or slate (a metamorphic rock), is very densely structured, absorbs little moisture, splits well and is used as thin slabs, usually dark grey to black. Even though it barely resists abrasion it can also be used as a floor covering. The material responds to surface damage by splitting off (individual layers of the material are worn away), and so remains homogeneous.

Texture

Natural stone occurs in a wide variety of individual colours and textures and responds to weathering by discolouring and wearing away to a greater or lesser extent. Textures flowing into each other across stone slabs create a homogeneous overall architectural picture. High colour contrasts generate a sense of structured vigour. The general impression it makes largely resists ageing, contrasting with weathered detail. › Fig. 27

Surface
treatment

The desired effect is achieved by the treatment of the stone's surface. Rough stone that has scarcely been worked at all presents an archaic aesthetic. Fractured edges, and the marks left by splitting, cutting and blasting, are reminders of the material's origins and extraction. More refined techniques such as pointing (a hammering technique), comb chiselling (a technique that uses a toothed chisel), bush hammering (roughening with a toothed hammer), sanding and polishing give the stone particular characteristics. Rough surfaces provide evidence of the processes undergone and contribute to the natural stone's massive, archaic appearance. If stone is polished, its texture is in the foreground, and it does not seem to get grimy, or to age. › Fig. 26

Jointing

Jointing natural stone derives from the stone formats available. These extend from untreated, round rubblestone for Cyclopean masonry, via square-cut stones of various sizes for masonry with irregular course, to finely hewn blocks for ashlar work, and polished or bevelled slabs for curtain façades. The character of the surface produced can be determined by emphasizing or concealing the joints. The more evenly coloured the joint and the stone are, the less the building is seen as a living structure and more as an apparently monolithic surface. The darker the joint, the more the stone used seems to stand out and glow. › Fig. 25

Fig. 27:
Ageing in a natural stone façade

Fig. 28:
Coursed masonry

Fig.29:
Concrete with wooden plank structure, exposed aggregate concrete, fibreglass concrete

CONCRETE

> 🔲

Concrete is the universal building material of our age. It has marked the development of 20th-century architecture decisively. It is an ambivalent material: used in liquid form, it is valued for its strength as artificial stone. Outwardly it shows the formwork rather than its own structure. Some people like concrete for its purist aesthetic, others find it brutal and inhuman.

Production

The mixture of cement, aggregates and water determines the properties of concrete. The cement acts as the binder, the water is present so that it can set, and the aggregates cut down the amount of cement needed and determine density, strength, thermal conductivity and heat storage capacity. Typical concrete has a high gross density, great surface hardness and great strength. The usual aggregate is gravel. The structure of large and small granules is calculated to create as few cavities as possible. The gravel will be completely enveloped by the cement and bound to it non-positively.

> 🔲

The smaller granule sizes help the concrete to flow more easily.

Aggregates

The properties of the concrete are determined by the aggregates. Normal concrete has high thermal conductivity and heat storage capacities. Thermal conductivity can be significantly reduced by changing the aggregates, for example by using expanded clay, particularly porous clay balls

🔲
\\ Hint:
Concrete is made from inorganic materials and is non-homogeneous. Essentially it is stone that can be moulded, and can be produced in any shape required, like ceramics (see page 54), and worked like natural stone (see page 39).

🔲
\\ Hint:
The water-cement ratio (w/c) defines the proportion of water and cement as a percentage. If the w/c ratio is less than 0.6, concrete that is impermeable to water can be produced. Concrete can thus be used in a loadbearing capacity, as well as taking over the function of damp-proofing.

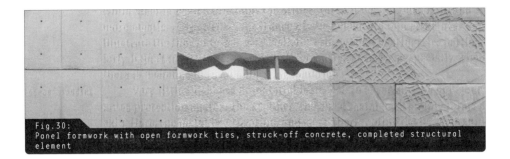

or wood chips. Thermal conductivity can be reduced further by introducing air pores as an insulation device. This is done by means of blowing agents, which make the concrete rise like a cake. The result is called aerated concrete. Chemical substances can also be added to make the fresh concrete easier to work; or colour pigments to dye the concrete.

Processing

The concrete loses volume while setting, and shrinks. To prevent cracks, sections to be concreted are defined and joints – or dummy joints, which are indicated on the surface only – are used as a "predetermined breaking point". The pressure of the liquid concrete, which has no independent loadbearing capacity during processing, has to be absorbed by a secondary structure. The formwork must be designed to the appropriate dimensions. To prevent vertical sections of the formwork from bulging, formwork ties are passed through the building component to be concreted and so the two sides of the formwork are attached to each other non-positively. They leave visible traces in the finished concrete. The surface of the shuttering and its joint pattern, as well as the formwork ties, define the texture of the visible concrete. › Fig. 30

Formwork

Fair-face concrete is the negative of its formwork. Sanded, rough or sandblasted timbers, › Fig. 29 left coated or uncoated formwork panels in wood, metal or plastic offer a wide variety of design possibilities. The internal structure of the concrete can also be revealed. The formwork surfaces can be treated with substances that slow down the setting process. If the surface is then sprayed with water, the gravel inside is revealed: the result is called exposed aggregate concrete, or washed concrete. › Fig. 29 centre The surface can be sanded or struck off subsequently to show the internal structure of the concrete. › Fig. 29 right Concrete can also be used entirely without a surface of its own by using permanent formwork, which simply remains in place at the end of the concreting process.

Reinforced concrete

As a simple mixture, concrete has little tensile strength, so if it is used structurally it will always be reinforced concrete. Reinforcing steel is introduced into the concrete at the points where loads have to be absorbed.

The lowest possible level of concrete covering is always planned to protect the steel against corrosion from the alkaline pH of the concrete. Concrete and steel also work together well because the two materials have almost the same coefficient of expansion. Textiles, or carbon or plastic fibres may also be used for reinforcement; these will reduce the amount of covering concrete needed and thus make it possible to produce particularly slender components. Elephant grass (Miscanthus) is a reinforcement that regrows. As a plant that grows very quickly, its cells store a great deal of minerals, which help to form a non-positive bond with the cement. This reinforcement inside the concrete makes the initially non-directional concrete into a directional compound material. Its loadbearing capacity can be influenced by moulding or by the statical height of the structure. Intelligent moulding, corresponding with the flow of forces in the concrete, opens up new design possibilities and can reduces the quantities of materials required considerably. › Fig. 31

Recycling

Concrete stands for durability. Its real useful life is determined by the particular way in which it is processed. The non-positive bond of steel and concrete makes it a compound material. It is hard to introduce concrete into a recycling programme, as the most of the energy is tied up in the chemical process of hardening the cement. Meaningful, complete recycling of a building component often fails because of the monolithic building methods used for concrete.

Fig.31:
Circular loadbearing structure with ribs

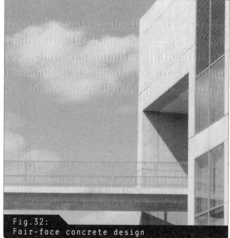

Fig.32:
Fair-face concrete design

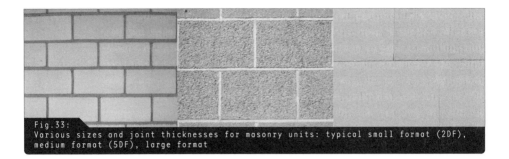

Fig.33:
Various sizes and joint thicknesses for masonry units: typical small format (2DF),
medium format (5DF), large format

MINERAL-BONDED MASONRY UNITS

> 🖉

Stone and massive building methods are usually associated with natural stone and bricks. But for some time now these materials have been complemented by mineral-bonded masonry units: calcium silicate units are made from lime, and concrete units from cement. Perforations can reduce weight, and embossing can structure the surface of the units. > Fig. 35 Such masonry units have come to be a common resource in the building industry, because they are readily available, and because of the ease with which they can be worked and processed, especially as they have a low gross density and high strength levels.

Production and
properties

Masonry units are hardened under steam pressure at average temperatures of 160 to 200 °C in autoclaves (gastight closed pressure containers). This production method means that they shrink very little, and the products are consistent in quality and dimensions. Masonry units are generally not sensitive to moisture: in fact, their surfaces absorb it from the air and release it back into the air again. This also has a positive effect on the

> 🖉

interior climate, but is undesirable in outdoor use. The binding agent used reinforces (e.g. in the case of gypsum or lime) or reduces (e.g. cement) this property. Calcium silicate external facing units are therefore impregnated. Masonry units also show high capillary forces, i.e. they absorb liquids. For this reason seals and horizontal insulating courses in rising wall have to be planned and executed very carefully when using masonry units.

🖉

\\Hint:
Like concrete (see page 42), masonry units with
mineral binding agents consist of inorganic
mineral material. They can be jointed like
ceramics and bricks (see page 54) or natural
stone (see page 39).

🖉

\\Hint:
The moisture-related properties of masonry
units can be used outdoors as floor coverings,
to reduce sealing. Particularly porous cement
units are produced to allow precipitation to
soak through into the subsoil.

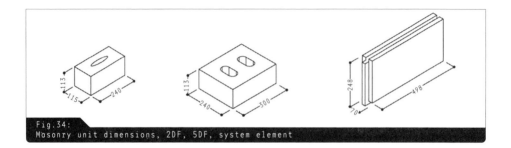

Aggregates

The choice of aggregates makes it possible to change the properties of the units, especially those of concrete masonry units. According to the type of aggregate, it is possible to produce lightweight concrete unit (pumice or expanded clay), granulated blast-furnace slag units (slag), or aerated concrete units (CO_2 as blowing agent). All these reduce the weight and thermal conductivity of the units. However, the units' surface hardness is reduced with their weight, which is an argument against using them for exposed surfaces (e.g. as fair-face masonry). Masonry units thus seldom develop their own properties as a wall material, and tend to be hidden under rendered surfaces.

Unit formats

Weight reduction makes it possible to increase the format of the commercially produced units. A workman's hand used to be the scale for bricks, but now they are sized according to how much a worker or a mechanical lifting device can handle, in order to speed the building process up further. But the formats are still largely based on the rules for brick masonry; larger formats do have their own sizes, however, derived from the structural quality of the material (high compression strength, low tensile bending strength), or from the customary spatial dimensions. › Fig. 34

Jointing

The units' high dimensional stability is the basis for format enlargement. Precise manufacturing processes can reduced the number of compensating joints needed. High precision compatibility means that joints can be thinner. › Fig.36 For interior use, this development is so far advanced

\\ Hint:
Further information on masonry unit formats and masonry structures can be found in *Basics Masonry Construction* by Nils Kummer, Birkhäuser Publishers, Basel 2007.

that only horizontal joints are needed. The kerf is then replaced with a mortar-free vertical joint with tongue and groove. › Fig. 33 right

For bricks, the joint is typically still recessed, for stone, the joint is protected from driving rain and other weathering, but for masonry units with mineral binders, especially calcium silicate units, the joints also help to protect the vulnerable edges of the units, so they should not be recessed. This means that masonry units always look flatter than comparable bricks, and their material depth shows only at the corners. This reduces the monolithic impression made by individual units, but for buildings with simple cubatures the monolithic impression from a distance can even be enhanced. › Fig. 36

This quality of flatness can be enhanced even further in the interior. Sometimes only very narrow joints are needed because of reduced thermal expansion as well. Masonry units with a ground surface, "terrazzo tiles", show the internal structure of the material on the surface. Essentially, all known techniques for natural stone and concrete can also be used for surface treatment.

Recycling   Masonry units are well suited to recycling regardless of material. The units are separated after use by detaching the jointing material and can then be reused as they are. It is essential that the jointing material is not as strong as the unit, as otherwise the unit will break first and cannot be used again. Particularly light units are not strong enough either, and become non-reusable materials. Mortar-free jointing (tongue and groove) makes a major contribution to reusability.

Fig.35:
Embossed concrete masonry units

Fig.36:
Concrete masonry units

Fig.37:
Section and top view of plasterboard, cement fibreboard, mineral cement board

BOARDS WITH MINERAL BINDERS

> 🗋

> 🗋

Classification
by binding agent

Properties

Boards with mineral binders are a typical material for interior cladding. Such boards have become an almost universal surface for lightweight wall and ceiling structures because they can easily be scored, sawn, cut, drilled and milled. Plasterboard is the most common, but there are also cement fibreboards, wood wool boards, mineral-bonded chipboards, fibrous plasterboards and perlite wallboards.

These boards can be classified as plaster or cement boards according to the binding agent used. Plaster sets rapidly when used for bonding, and is thus suitable for making boards by extrusion. The very fluid plaster is enclosed in cardboard on both sides, and then shaped under pressure. The strip of board is endless at first, then cut to size. Micropores in the plaster structure establish the material's absorbent properties: it absorbs moisture well and thus makes it possible to control interior humidity well.

Cement bonds noticeably more slowly. It is therefore unsuitable for an extrusion process, and has to be pressed into shape. Cement-bonded boards are therefore stronger than the plaster versions. The material can also be waterproofed. The strength of cement boards can be exploited for loadbearing and reinforcement.

Despite the boards being relatively thin, the material can be used structurally if it is reinforced to withstand lateral and tensile forces.

🗋
\\Hint:
Mineral-bonded boards have an inorganic mineral composition, a non-homogeneous structure, and are used similarly to timber products (see page 36).

🗋
\\Hint:
The DIN EN 520 standard changed the old DIN 18180 designation standard wallboard to plasterboard.

sealing with
reinforcement strip

corner with edge
protection

Fig.38:
Fitting plasterboard

› 🗍

Fibrous materials are used almost exclusively as aggregates; glass fabric is also used for perlite wallboards. This kind of reinforcement is placed on the outside, in order to develop its own statical height. Plasterboard goes a step further. It is reinforced by the cardboard that covers it on both sides, making it very strong but light, and reducing its thermal conductivity. A great deal of performance is lost, however, if the cardboard surface is weakened or damaged. The surface lie of the cardboard makes the plasterboard more efficient in one axis, so it is available in rectangular form. Untreated plasterboard is vulnerable to water. › Fig. 37

Edge design

Plasterboard was developed to act as support for an overlay or top-coat (e.g. wallpaper or paint). This means that areas without visible joints are needed, with production joints that are able to accommodate lateral expansion invisibly. Plasterboard is therefore supplied with various edge patterns optimized for special applications, and sealed with or without joint reinforcement after assembly. › Fig. 38

Architecture
for interior
spaces

Plasterboard represents the idea of a material without any visible properties. The plane of the material and its texture retreat completely in favour of other materials or the way a space is perceived as a whole. White architecture of the kind used in Richard Meier's buildings would be inconceivable without plasterboard. › Fig. 39

🗍

\\Hint:
Perlite is a natural, hydrous, glass-like
stone. Heating evaporates the water content
and enlarges the volume of the material up to
20 times.

Mineral-bonded boards can also express a quite different, new material quality. Cement fibreboards are available in concrete grey for use on façades, and other colours are available as well, introduced into the cement as pigments. They are usually flat for façade use, but can also be corrugated for structural purposes. This increases their static height and thus the maximum span that can be achieved. They can be overlapped and assembled to form a continuous layer that is impervious to water.

The boards' surface properties also mean they can be used for sound-proofing; wood wool boards are a good example here. Their rough, open-pored surface scatters and absorbs sound. These rough, reasonably priced boards have a crude, technical aesthetic, and make fixings and built-in units stand out particularly. They combine well with mineral bonding agents and are thus also suitable for permanent formwork in service rooms or underground car parks. › Fig. 40

Mineral-bonded boards are not usually used structurally. They are easily replaced as planking for upright walls. The boards can be reclaimed without major material loss. Even so, their recycling quota is very low, as the material is very reasonably priced, and creates little or no toxic waste.

Fig.39:
Interior architecture

Fig.40:
Wood wool boards as ceiling cladding

Fig.41:
Terrazzo screed, tile screed, OSB screed

PLASTER AND SCREEDS

> 🏛

Plaster and screeds create large surface areas without joints. They protect the materials underneath from moisture, frost and fire, and act as load-distributing elements.

> 🖉

Screed

Screed is poured on site and hardens on contact. Like all mineral bonding materials, it shrinks while hardening, which means that cracks can form, so contraction joints should be planned. Setting times are also very important in the building process. It is usually possible to walk on a cement screed after 7 days, but it needs 28 days to reach its defined strength. Anhydrite and mastic asphalt screeds can be walked on considerably sooner. The elastic quality of bitumen means it can be applied more thinly, but can be joint-free over a wide area. It can also meet reduced soundproofing requirements without impact sound insulation, as it prevents structure-borne sound from being conducted.

Impact sound insulation

Impact sound-insulated screeds float in sheet form on elastic insulation. Insulation strips prevent sound from being transmitted via rising walls. Dry screed, made of plasterboard, for example, can be reused and is easy to replace. Terrazzo, tile and timber screed offer surfaces with distinctive material properties. > Fig. 41

🏛
\\ Hint:
Plaster and screeds are composed mainly of inorganic materials and are similar to concrete (see page 42) in the way they are treated. Their surfaces can be worked like natural stone (see page 39).

🖉
\\ Tip:
Plaster is a standard building material. It is worth taking advantage of the many surface variants of plaster, as this involves scarcely any more expense or effort, but makes it possible to create greater added value for the architecture.

Fig.42:
Various plaster surfaces

Plaster

Plaster protects the materials underneath it and provides homogeneous surfaces that can also be decorative. › Fig. 43 Technically speaking, two finishes are possible: on the one hand, plaster has an open-pored structure and can remove any moisture that may have penetrated the material underneath it. The plaster will then tend to be fragile, and is easily damaged; it is the weakest layer of the wall structure and requires constant care. On the other hand, plaster can form a particularly strong, dense surface that maintains its protective function for a considerable time. This finish is very easy to maintain in the first place, but if there is any defect the plaster has to be replaced completely, and the support is usually damaged in the process of removing the outer layer of plaster, as this is so strong.

Composition of plaster

The plasters available are classified according to the type of binder. Loam plaster can be used only as an undercoat and for interior work. Moisture-sensitive plaster is also used in interiors only, but is suitable for creative work and for fine stucco. Lime plaster types that are able to diffuse vapour range from soft air-hardening to hard hydraulic lime plasters. They are used as a water-inhibiting layer indoors and outdoors. Using cement as a binding agent makes it possible to produce capillary waterproof lime-cement and cement plasters for outdoor use. Special plasters such as renovation, fireproofing, acoustic, and thermal insulation plaster can be produced with the use of aggregates.

Plaster ground

It is essential that the plaster should adhere to its ground immediately, without becoming solid in its own right. Plaster can therefore be applied only up to a limited thickness. If the ground draws too much moisture out of the plaster, it will not solidify fully. If the substrate does not respond to moisture at all, only a low-level, non-positive bond can be established. The plaster ground is therefore often primed.

Plaster supports

If the plaster ground cannot guarantee adhesion, special plaster supports must be used. Plastic fabric mats or reeds then hold the plaster in position. The principle still works if the plaster support replaces a solid plaster ground. Wire meshing is then used to guarantee loadbearing capacity. Rabitz plastering of this kind has a degree of elasticity that makes it possible to damp down oscillation, and thus also deaden sound.

Design

Plaster has a function as part of the design, as well as offering protection. It creates a monolithic impression. The surface texture is discernible only from close to, when it becomes clear that the plaster is just an outer skin. › Fig. 44 This texture is based on the material and the application technique: the chosen process leaves marks as a result of the interplay between tools, additives and the hardening process. Surfaces of this kind can be determined by random factors in the distribution of the additives (gravel and sand), or the way the worker handles tools. Plaster can be coloured by painting or by penetration dyeing.

Texture

The first possible texture is created directly by the way the moist plaster is applied. It can be sprayed over large areas, or applied over small areas with a trowel or brush. Plaster that has dried slightly can be marked over large areas in free forms with a trowel, a wooden plank with a structured surface, or special combs and rollers. Shortly before the plaster dries out completely, the surface can be rubbed with a spongeboard for a particularly smooth finish. It is also possible to wash off the surface binder mask and allow the plaster additives to show. A stonemason's skills can also be used. › See chapter Natural stone Scraping off the surface of plaster, which is particularly rich in binding agents and tends to accumulate tension, makes it possible to create large areas free of shrinkage cracks. › Fig. 42

Fig.43:
Decorative façade design with plaster

Fig.44:
Plaster as a coating

Fig.45:
Various ceramics in use (pantile, brick, tile)

CERAMICS AND BRICKS

> ◧

Ceramics go back a very long way, with evidence available from the 4th century BC. Their name derives from the Greek "keramos", and means fired earth.

Clay as basic material

The basic material for ceramics is clay, which consists largely of hydrous aluminium compounds, and has a flat foliar structure that makes it plastically mouldable. The soft mass is pressed into a mould to create a "green tile". In today's extrusion presses, the mouthpiece can be changed to alter the cross section of the product; the extruded ribbon is cut to length according to the product size required.

Firing and properties

The product does not become water-resistant until it has been fired. The foliar clay structure fuses at a temperature of about 800 °C. The earthenware produced in this way has a high capillarity. From about 1200 °C the sintering process takes place: the aluminium compounds fuse to produce a vitreous structure. Cavities are surrounded, and the capillarity thus reduced to a minimum, giving a frostproof sintered product. Ceramics lose volume in the firing process. This cannot be predetermined, and means there are high dimension and product tolerances. Fired ceramics are subdivided into ordinary and fine ceramics by grain size and by the degree of porosity. > Fig. 45 They have high gross density, hardness, compressive strength and abrasion resistance. Like stone, they have low tensile strength.

◧
\\Hint:
Ceramics are composed of inorganic material. Their structure is similar to that of glass (see page 62). Bricks are used in similar ways to natural stone (see page 39) and mineral-bonded masonry units (see page 45).

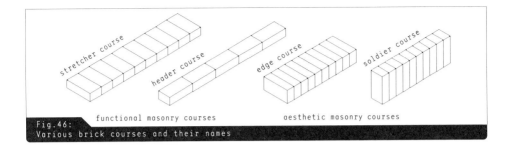

functional masonry courses   aesthetic masonry courses

Fig.46:
Various brick courses and their names

Surface colour and texture are produced by the moulding and firing process. An additional possibility is surface coating, where the product acquires a hard ceramic covering, the engobe. This then determines the hardness, smoothness and colour of the ceramics, and can seal the surface of earthenware, for example. Ceramics can also be treated using techniques such as flaming.

Brick

The dimensions of bricks are subject to a strict octametric system. Normal and thin formats, much used in fair-face masonry, have been replaced by large-format bricks or blocks when they will not be visible, although they use the same system of measurements so that the different wall courses can be matched. When designing a masonry building it is worth using the octametric system from the outset, so that any joints can be handled sensibly at a later stage. Bricks can only be pressure-loaded, so it is important to work out the pressure forces first of all when working with masonry.

Texture

The texture of brick masonry is determined by the jointing of the bricks, with stretcher and header courses keying the masonry together. › Fig. 46 The colour of the joint, the joint pattern and the way it is executed determine how the dimensions and material depth are perceived. The joint is often recessed, which reveals the depth of the masonry unit. In this way, an individual unit can develop a solid quality of its own, as well as the whole area of wall, and at the same time protect the joint against the weather. The usual joint thickness of 1 cm derives from the high tolerances in brick dimensions, and differences in shape can be compensated for by the joint design.

Solid
construction

Bricks are used in a variety of ways. New developments, featuring increasingly large formats and lower weights, have speeded up the building process. Low weights and low conductivity are also thermal protection requirements. To improve them, and to meet raised thermal protection requirements for façades with single-shell masonry, wood chips or polystyrene beads are mixed with the clay; these then create cavities when

55

the material is fired. The gross density can be further reduced by using extruder press cross sections with a high proportion of air chambers.

Facing masonry shell

If the typical visual effect of brick is to be combined with high thermal protection levels, an insulating layer must be planned in the interior of the wall. To avoid having to build two walls, the outer part of the wall is attached to the inner one. Only water-resistant, frost- and efflorescence-proof facing bricks or clinker bricks can be used for this purpose. The facing masonry shell is usually just one brick thick and is held in place by stainless steel masonry ties. The problem of apertures is that the lowest stones have to dissipate any compressive forces acting on them, either to beams or to specially suspended steel sections. Expansion joints should be allowed for every 5–12 m within the facing shell. › Fig. 47

Ceramic panels

Ceramic panels suspended on metal sections are also used for façades. They provide protection against the weather, and are very thin, thus considerably reducing the loads to be dissipated. The ceramic panels are not bound positively, but create a water run-off layer through overlapping and joints. Such façades seem light in contrast with the massive quality of masonry.

Roof tiles

Roof tiles follow a similar construction principle. Flat roof tiles such as the flat-tail need a high level of overlap and are used only on steep roofs. Roof tiles with overlapping lips can be laid at considerably lower pitches.
› Fig. 48

Recycling

Bricks, a material with high primary energy consumption and high durability, are suitable for product recycling provided they can be separated from the jointing mortar. Ceramic panels and roofing tiles that are used with open joints and without mortar are ideal for recycling and repairs.

Fig. 47:
Brick curtain façade

Fig. 48:
Courtyard housing estate in brick

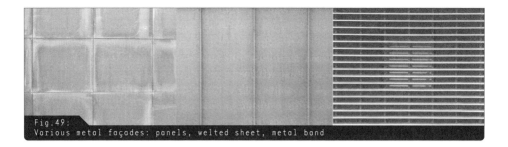

Fig.49:
Various metal façades: panels, welted sheet, metal band

METALS

The largest group of chemical elements, metals, are divided into heavy metals with a gross density of more than 4500 kg/m^3 (lead, copper, zinc, iron), and light metals with a low gross density (aluminium, magnesium). As iron is the metal most commonly used in building, an additional distinction is made between ferrous and non-ferrous metals.

> Properties

The special properties of metals are high density, high compressive and tensile strength, high melting point, high thermal and electric conductivity, a metallic sheen, and elasticity. Because these properties are derived from their crystalline structure, combining several metals (alloys) in a crystal lattice does not unite their properties, but creates a quite separate set. Small additions can therefore be used to set properties of alloys very precisely. There are 2000 known alloys of iron alone, including various qualities of stainless steel, which is weatherproof and retains its sheen permanently.

Iron and steel

Ferrous metals with a carbon content of less than two percent are known as steel. This is more elastic than iron, can be welded, and has a higher tensile strength. Because of their great strength and weight, iron and steel building components are geometrically optimized for static efficiency. The shape of I-girders or trapezoid sheets provides information about areas of structural use and minimizes the amount of material used. Iron oxidizes, and therefore needs to be protected from contact with the air.

\\Hint:
Further information on roof tiles can be found in *Basics Roof Construction* by Tanja Brotrück, Birkhäuser Publishers, Basel 2007.

\\Hint:
Metals are inorganic materials; they have a crystalline structure and are smelted, in a similar way to glass (see page 62).

57

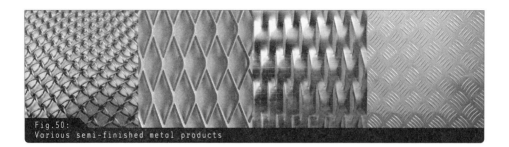

Fig.50:
Various semi-finished metal products

Zinc, copper
and lead

Zinc and copper are weatherproof and easy to work, and thus used for façade cladding, covering sheets and roof drainage components. In building, silvery zinc is almost always used in the form of an alloy with a low titanium content (titanium zinc). This reduces thermal expansion, improves elasticity and makes the material weldable. Copper gleams reddish-brown, and is much sought after in building for its appearance and good weather resistance. Matte-grey lead is not strong; it can be cut with shears and shaped by hand. Lead is used for roofs, particularly for parts that would be very laborious or expensive to make mechanically out of other metals. However, lead is toxic: abrasion leads to its accumulating in the food chain.

Aluminium

Aluminium has a low gross density and is therefore a lightweight metal. It can be used wherever reduced weight and weatherproof qualities are important, especially for façade elements. Even a natural oxide layer makes the material weatherproof; technical oxidization (anodizing) can reinforce this layer and introduce colour.

Yielding

One particular temperature-dependent property of metals is called yielding. Metals respond to forces acting on them by plastic deformation accompanied by a sudden loss of loadbearing capacity. Although metals are not combustible, yielding means that they must be effectively protected from fire.

> ♀

> \\Important:
> Loadbearing metal sections must be protected
> from fire. Fireproof cladding or special paints
> are used for this purpose; such paints foam
> up in case of fire and create a protective
> layer.

Only precious metals like silver, gold and platinum have such a low reactive capacity that they appear in their pure form in nature. All other metals are present as ore in compounds of carbon, oxygen or sulphur, and have to be separated from these before production. Damage to the landscape when mining ore, and the amount of energy needed to extract metal from ore, create high levels of environmental pollution and expense. The costs and benefits of using metal must therefore be weighed up with due care. On the other hand, reuse of metals has made very great progress. Tying them into material cycles improves their environmental impact. › see chapter Material requirements, Environmental pollution

Base metals react with atmospheric gases and water. When two metals touch, the less noble metal will pass electrons on to the more noble one whether this is desirable or not, and only the less noble metal corrodes. As well as having a colour of its own, the corroded layer may have particular properties in relation to water. In some metals like aluminium, copper, zinc and lead, this produces a stable, protective structure that envelops the metal core. For copper and copper alloys such as bronze, a grey to green patina, sometimes uneven, forms over time. › Fig. 54 Weatherproof steel produces a protective layer of reddish-brown rust, although this lasts only if the surrounding air is not too moist. › Fig. 49 left Sheet metal that already has a patina is available on the market so that this patina can be exploited deliberately.

Normal iron does not form a stable protective layer, but rusts. Paint or powder coatings are therefore used to prevent it coming into contact

Fig.51:
Loadbearing structure for a bridge

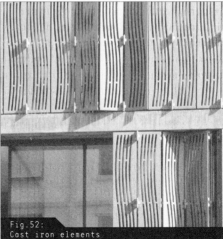

Fig.52:
Cast iron elements

with air and water and corroding. This may mean that it loses its special effect. Galvanization provides a protective metallic coating that restores the metallic appearance.

We distinguish between hot and cold shaping processes. In cold shaping the structure of the atoms within the metal lattice is rearranged, thereby increasing the metal's strength. Rolling produces simple sheets. Commercial steel girders and shaped metal sheets are rolled into the desired form over several stages. Extrusion produces components with complicated cross sections. Here, a solid metal bar, usually aluminium or another non-ferrous metal, is pushed through a template under high pressure. Drawing produces wire and rods, and thus also structural steel for reinforcing concrete. Forging using a hammer and anvil can be either a cold or a hot process. Moulded parts and complicated structural connecting elements are cast in a negative mould. Tin and copper alloys are suitable for producing particularly fine cast parts, and cast steel for complex connecting elements that need to withstand high loads in steel and timber construction.

Mechanical
processes

Mechanical processes include a wide range of chip-producing (subtractive process producing shavings) techniques: drilling, milling, sanding, turning, sandblasting, filing and sawing. Bending, edging, stamping and welting produce new shapes mechanically. Shaping and mechanical processing can also produce semi-finished metal products such as stamped sheets, expanded metals, metal meshes, and many other products. › Fig. 50

Connections

Metal parts can be connected temporarily or permanently. Screws, nails, rivets, pins, welts and clamps are temporary connections. Permanent connections are created by various welding techniques, soldering and gluing.

› 🛇

Constructions

Metals are highly efficient and can therefore be used in very slender forms. They can be pressure or tension loaded. Ferrous metals are generally used for structural sections because of their strength. Cast iron carries the imprint of the mould and can stand very high compressive loads,

🛇
\\Hint:
To improve the reusability of metals,
structures should be easy to dismantle and
separate from non-metal building materials.

while steel is easier to mould for structural and design purposes, and is more elastic. › Fig. 52 The appearance of steel elements and structures can illustrate the flow of forces very well. Here, bases and bearings are particularly important. They demonstrate the transfer of forces, especially when there is a change in the loadbearing material. › Fig. 51

Façade cladding   Very little thickness of material is needed to cover an area and guarantee protection against the weather. The sheet metal used simply forms a skin. Here, the metal is a covering, and a weatherproofing device. Self-supporting façade elements in steel or aluminium can be produced flat, but to save material and weight they are usually shaped, i.e. edged or convex. Highly elastic metals such as copper or titanium-zinc can be shaped when cold, and are therefore commonly used for façade cladding. When used flat, the sheets can be welted on site (bent overlapping), and can then cover almost any surface shape and follow it in their welted form. › Fig. 53

Metals can also be designed to admit light into buildings when used as façade cladding, in the form of expanded metals, aerated metals or metal mesh. The metallic sheen can play a role, as it emphasizes the particular properties of the material, and can be used to direct light into the depths of the space.

Fig.53:
Titanium-zinc cladding

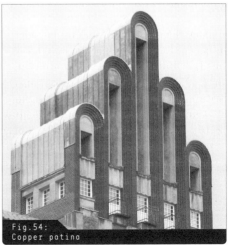

Fig.54:
Copper patina

GLASS

As a transparent building material, glass plays a key part in architecture, because its invisibility means that it can almost dissolve the material quality of the building. It forms an effective spatial conclusion, while fulfilling the basic human need for daylight.

Properties

Like all materials, glass absorbs radiation. This takes place in the non-visible part of the spectrum, and so glass appears permeable to light. As it cools quickly in manufacture, a crystalline structure can form. It is thus an amorphous building material. Glass is dense (2490 kg/m³), hard and brittle, abrasion-resistant, and has high compressive strength. Because it is so brittle, and its surface tension resembles that of water, it can withstand little tensile and bending load. The surface of the glass is brittle as well, and it can therefore be cut by scoring the surface, which is then broken along the score line.

Composition

Quartz sand is the principal raw material of glass. Simple building glass, also called normal glass, is made from silicon dioxide, sodium oxide and calcium oxide. The particular composition determines the properties of the glass. › Tab. 7

Float glass process

Glass used for building is usually made by the float glass process. Glass is floated on a bath of molten tin. The lighter molten glass floats to the surface, where it slowly cools down and solidifies. During this process it is slowly drawn from the completely level bath. The stream of molten glass forms an endless sheet, which is immediately cut into transport

\\Hint:
Glass consists of inorganic material, and is amorphous. Plastics share many of its properties (see page 66), and its manufacture is similar to that of metals (see page 57).

\\Hint:
Glass is dimensioned not according to its strength, but in terms of the likelihood of breaking. Thus it is actually overdimensioned.

lengths of up to 7.5 m. The glass produced in this way has a high surface quality and is eminently suitable for further processing.

Pressed/rolled glass

Glass can also be shaped by rollers or presses. Rolled glass may be decorative and has ornaments or structures; safety glass with a built-in wire element; or figured glass. These products are U-shaped in cross section and can be installed to be self-supporting. If they are installed vertically, an endless band of glass can be created.

Cast glass

In casting, the molten glass is poured into a mould and hardens there. Glass bricks consist of two glass half-shells pressed together. These bricks can be jointed like masonry. › Fig. 55

Foam glass/ glass fibres

High-quality pressure- and waterproof transparent insulating materials can be made from glass or recycled glass by a foaming process. Glass fibres are produced in many versions to conduct light and for reinforcement purposes.

Glass finishing

Before being used for construction, glass is often processed further as required, for example by thermal treatment, surface coating or laminating. Thermal treatment produces a particular surface tension. The result, toughened safety glass, does not form sharp edges when it breaks. Heat-treated glass breaks into larger pieces than toughened safety glass. Enamelling (melting a glass powder on to the surface), fusing (melting on pieces of glass), obscuring processes, or screen printing can create partially transparent, translucent or opaque surfaces.

Semi-finished glass products

Laminated safety glass and insulating glass are produced by combining various types of glass. For laminated safety glass, several layers of glass are bonded together with plastic film. In case of breakage, this has a residual loadbearing capacity, which makes the glass useful for statical purposes, up to the level of bullet-proofing. Insulating and thermal

Tab.7:
Selected types of glass and their uses

Glass type	Changed composition	Effect	Use
Borosilicate glass	Added boric oxide	Heat resistant	Fireproof glass
Quartz glass	Added silicon dioxide	Heat resistant, high transmission	Energy gain systems
Lead glass	Added lead dioxide	High light refraction	Lenses, decorative glass
Clear glass	Added iron oxide	Particularly colour-neutral glass	Façades
Coloured glass	Added iron oxide	Green to blue tinge	Decorative glass
	Added chromium oxide	Light green tinge	Decorative glass
	Added copper oxide	Red tinge	Decorative glass
	Added cobalt oxide	Deep blue tinge	Decorative glass
	Added silver oxide	Yellow tinge	Decorative glass

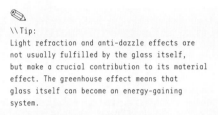
insulation glass combines two or more glasses with a gap that consider-ably reduces the glass's thermal conductivity, especially when filled with inert gases. Coatings can reflect radiant heat; solar control glass reflects some of the solar radiation outwards, and thermal insulation glass main-tains the ambient temperature. Special glasses for improved soundproof-ing and fireproofing are available, and adaptive glasses accommodate to their environment.

Glass fixing

It is important that glass is mounted without tensions to avoid ten-sile and bending forces. It can be supported along a line by pressing or bonding, and at certain points by chocking (wedges in a frame), spider ele-ments (multi-foot elements for combining panes of glass), or clamps.

Transparency and reflection

Glass's transparency is always in the foreground, along with the desire to fix it as unobtrusively as possible, so that the whole loadbearing

Fig.56:
Transparent façade

Fig.57:
Translucent façade

structure dissolves visually. A typical post-and-rail façade can be executed in glass, or replaced by cable systems. › Fig. 56 But in fact it is impossible to dematerialize the architecture with glass. The eye cannot equate shaded areas in the depths of a space with the outside space. › see p. 12 The rhythm of day and night means that this relationship is always weighted differently for the building. From the darker side, the perception is better up to the point where the building is translucent from one side only. The other surface of the glass begins to reflect its surroundings. Reflecting glass surfaces can also be created deliberately. Buildings then make less of an effect, or blur into the sky. Mirror surfaces can be disturbing for viewers, because they sense they could be watched without their knowing.

Translucency
and layering

Partially transparent materials can mute the imbalance brought about by the day-night relationship, as only shadowy effects are created. In such cases, a façade becomes a functional print of the building in the outdoor space, any movements are perceived, and so it is possible to see how the building is used. The material behind is obvious as a layered structure, without having to reveal all its properties in terms of texture and design. This sketchy view through the building fires the viewers' expectations, which can either be met or contradicted subsequently. The extent of the view through the building can be reduced so that only light passes through, i.e. it seems translucent. This reinforces the spatial impression along with the expressive quality of the materials on which the light is shining. › Fig. 57

Fig.58:
Glass reflection

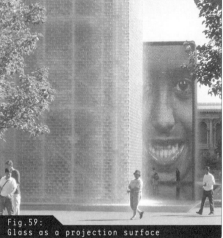

Fig.59:
Glass as a projection surface

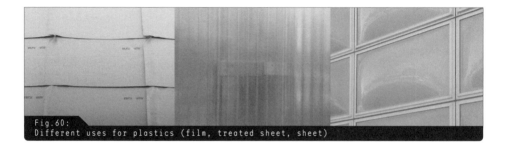

Fig.60:
Different uses for plastics (film, treated sheet, sheet)

PLASTICS

Plastics are the most recent group of materials in building history. Their development from natural raw materials such as rubber started in the mid-19th century, but their use in architecture did not reach its provisional peak until the futuristic designs of the 1960s. Plastics had a poor reputation until the late 1980s because of technical faults in the material, but this has now largely been overcome. They are an up-to-date material for many building components, and act unobtrusively as technical materials.

Properties

Although their properties can vary considerably, the following holds for almost all plastics: they have low gross density and thermal conductivity, a high coefficient of thermal expansion, high tensile strength, and are resistant to water and many chemicals. There are restrictions relating to the long-term service temperature: if it is too high they lose their strength; if it is too low they become brittle. Three groups can be distinguished, according to macromolecular structure.

Thermoplastics

Thermoplastic macromolecules tangle around themselves without forming chemical bonds. As the temperature increases, they first become elastic, then start to melt. Their elastic properties are useful for sealing

\\Hint:
Plastics are organic compounds, but they have no defined structural composition. They are an important raw material for textiles, similar to metals in the way they can be shaped (see page 57) and to glass in their structure (see page 62) and can also be worked similarly to timber products (see page 36).

\\Hint:
Plastics are sometimes known by trade names, details of their composition, or an abbreviation according to composition and manufacture. The abbreviations offer the quickest and simplest way of making comparisons.

Fig.61:
Surfaces of semi-finished plastic products

> 📎

and protecting strips in polyethylene (PE), PVC or ETFE strips, or for floor coverings. › Fig. 60 left Amorphous thermoplastics such as PMMA (acrylic glass) are transparent, hard and brittle. › Fig. 60 left Polycarbonate (PC), which has crystalline as well as tangled structures, is stronger, but only translucent. The strength and hardness of thermoplastics is used to raise the air volume to an extreme degree by foaming, thus increasing their insulation properties, e.g. for polystyrene (XPS / EPS) or polyurethane (PUR).

Thermosets   Thermosets have three-dimensional cross-linking. They are produced under pressure, at a high temperature and using chemical additives (hardeners). In particular, they include the epoxy resins (EP), used for resistant coatings and bonding. Combined with glass, carbon or aramide fibres they produce highly efficient materials for loadbearing structures.

Elastomers   Elastomers consist of cross-linked low-density molecular chains. Rubber is used for floor coverings and insulation strips, because it wears well and resists chemicals, and its elastic properties provide sound insulation. Silicones (SI) behave similarly to elastomers, although their structure is based on silicon rather than carbon. Their high temperature stability makes them preferred seals indoors and outdoors, and they are suitable as façade jointing mastics.

Production   Plastics are generally produced from mineral oil, but they can also be made from renewable raw materials. A basic material is initially produced, usually in granular form, and then moulded into a semi-finished product. Plastics can be prepared industrially using additives to give them individual properties, and they can be produced in different colours.

Shaping methods   Shaping methods include extrusion (shaped by a mouthpiece in a press), injection moulding (pressed into moulds under pressure and at a high temperature), calendaring (rolling and stamping), expansion and foaming. Extrusion presses can produce multi-chamber sheets or sections with cross sections of almost unlimited complexity. › Fig. 60 centre Flat strips and sheets are rolled out; their surfaces can be stamped. Some sheets are formed with construction in mind, e.g. wide-span corrugated sheeting.

Floor coverings can be specially surfaced to increase slip-resistance. › Fig. 61, centre right Injection moulding allows considerable design freedom, although it must be borne in mind that the product has to be removed from the mould after hardening. It is possible to produce moulded parts like handles in this way, as well as structured sheets and much else. › Fig. 61 left

Post-processing   A special technique for thermoplastics is thermoforming, also known as deep drawing. Here, the thermoplastic is heated, pressed over a special mound or drawn into shape in a vacuum. › Fig. 60 right Free forms, such as for designing large areas, can be created in foamed plastics by computer-aided three-dimensional mills; such products are used as underlay for solid coverings. › Fig. 63

Jointing   Flat sheets are mounted like panes of glass. › see p. 62 If sheets have been shaped, their edges are usually formed so that the sheets are joined non-positively on an axis one below the other. Corrugated sheets form a water-bearing layer by overlapping. › Fig. 60 centre Strips and films can be joined by gluing, vulcanizing or welding. Overlaps or welded seams protrude above the surface. › Fig. 60 left Welding can be done crudely by raising the temperature and exerting pressure, but it can also be tightly controlled, as in high-frequency welding. The ends are usually given metal clamps.

Recycling   The primary energy content of plastics is usually low, as is their durability in relation to other building materials. Thermoplastics that have been used particularly homogeneously can be cleaned and then reused. But the most common type of reuse is incineration to produce energy.

Fig.62:
Polycarbonate façade

Fig.63:
Bus stop in Hoofddorp

Fig.64:
Various textiles

TEXTILES AND MEMBRANES

> [image]

Human culture has known textile structures from its earliest days. Tents were the nomads' ideal accommodation : they were easy to transport, could be pitched and struck within a short period, and were easy to produce. Textiles, and particularly carpets, became the simplest way of defining rooms in these cultures. Textiles are still used in today's building, although they are used differently.

Production

The term "textile" comes from the Latin and means woven or plaited, regardless of the material used. If the raw materials used for textiles are arranged within a two-dimensional structure, they are known as woven fabric. Unordered, homogenous structures in which the fibres are tangled up with each other are known as felts and fleeces. Their three-dimensional structure makes them suitable for construction as well, for separating parts of a construction or providing sound insulation, for example.

Basic materials used

Natural fibres spun into threads are the most usual basic materials for textiles. If tactile properties and moisture resistance are particularly important, cotton and wool are the major raw materials. If the textile has to be particularly hardwearing (e.g. for floor coverings), rougher fibres such as coconut or sisal are used. These natural fibres can be attacked by fungus, bacteria or insects. Artificial fibres are usually tougher; those made of polyesters or nylon are particularly resistant to tearing. If coated, they can

> [image]

[image]

\\Hint:
Textiles and membranes do not have a defined composition or structure. They can be produced from natural fibres, plastics (see page 66) or metals (see page 57).

[image]

\\Hint:
All textiles can be chemically treated or coated to improve their properties. However, these layers may contain toxic substances. Labels can provide a certain degree of transparency about the production processes.

Fig.65:
Various uses for membranes and textiles (sun-, sight- and dazzle-screen)

be waterproof and yet open to vapour diffusion. Fabrics can also be made from metal wire, in steel or copper, for example. These are very strong, and can be woven to a high degree of translucency.

Properties   Textiles are soft, and warm and pleasant to the touch. They acquire their properties from the way in which they are made and from the basic material. If their prime function is not an aesthetic one, they are known as technical textiles. They can be used to weatherproof an area, but can take only tensile loads.

Joining   Textiles are usually sewn together. Seams can be treated artfully, be emphasized by the colour of the seam, or be particularly unobtrusive if they are sewn on the reverse side. If textiles are to function as stretched surfaces, the support must be linear. Point supports are weak points, so the forces generated have to be distributed over a wide area. Eyes, darts and reinforcements can be used for this purpose. Straps or guys can be used to dissipate forces. Textiles can be deployed in a variety of ways, but those listed below are probably the most common.

Membranes   Translucent membranes use very little material but offer good weatherproofing and are suitable for controlling daylight. They work particularly well for temporary structures, in the form of tensile-loaded two-dimensional structures. Fabrics, which can dissipate forces through warp and weft (the manufacturers' name for threads turned through 90°), are particularly suitable for this application. Plastic films can be used as an alternative to textiles. Membrane structures require three-dimensionally curved surface geometries, to generate tensile forces throughout. Curves running counter to each other (e.g. saddle forms or hyperbolic paraboloids) stabilize the membrane without additional construction. › Fig. 66 But membranes are always curved at their extremities: if lines were kept straight, the tensile forces would soar almost infinitely, or the membrane would tend to flutter because of the reduction in tensile forces. So only a few points have to be defined for load distribution. Meanwhile, surfaces that are curved in the same direction, like domes or cylinders, need a secondary structure, whose support points and lines then determine their form. › Fig. 67

Because of their low weight, membranes are also well suited for adaptable structures like roofs whose folding or expansion mechanism has to match the volume of the folded membrane. Thin films and coated glass fibre fabrics are unsuitable for use here, because they are insufficiently crease-resistant.

Multi-layered membranes can provide heat insulation and thus also be used for stationary structures. › Fig. 66 Here, they achieve ratings between 2.7 and 0.8 W/m^{2}K. However, allowances must be made for leakage, so the volumes must have a constant supply of air. With regulated ventilation, controllable solar protection systems in double- and triple-layer membrane constructions can also be produced. The individual membranes are printed with staggered solar protection patterns; changes to the membrane volumes regulates the way these patterns relate to the position of the sun. › Fig. 65 left

Carpets and felts are among the most common floor coverings, because they offer a high level of comfort in terms of tactile experience and room acoustics, and make the dwelling feel cosier. If fabrics are used to cover seats or handles, the substructure is covered with cushioning made of a foam material or felt, to emphasize the softness and warmth of the material. Textiles are also suitable for flexible built-in structures and curtains, which can be used to regulate the extent to which a room can be seen into or out of, thus completing the overall architectural effect. › Fig. 65 right When closed, they present a translucent surface, and when open, the fall of their folds creates a three-dimensional effect.

Fig.66:
Multi-layer membrane façade

Fig.67:
Textile barrel roof construction

DESIGNING WITH MATERIALS

Designing means developing something unbuilt into something built. Its particular quality is that the building is not there – or not there yet. No one can live in it, no one can be aware of it. And yet it does already exist in the form of sketches, drawings, models and texts. The ground plan, the view of the façade, shape and colour, expression and atmosphere, wood or stone, concrete or steel: the whole building is there before us, devised and designed. It is there – and yet not there. Building is inseparably linked with material. Its material quality is apparent even at the design stage – sometimes only in a shadowy form, sometimes very precisely. It is the material that determines the effect the architecture will make: architecture for its part is an inherent harmony of task, form and material.

> 🗎

Design strategies

But how does the designer come to give expressive and conclusive form to his or her material? Essentially, two strategies can be distinguished: the material can be the starting-point for a design, or the design process initially takes place quite independently of any ideas about materials. If the materials are the first decision, the design and structure emerge from their properties and significance. › see p. 31/32 A design that emerges independently of the material must be translated into material

> 🗎

terms later, which can sometimes mean adapting the design.

GENERAL CONDITIONS

Context

Design and material are always tied in with a specific context, which is explored at the beginning of the design process. The surroundings are the most important general condition: in particular, the buildings surrounding the new one, their scale, proportions, and of course the quality of their

---

🗎

\\Hint:
Even if the first sketches and design ideas do not have to carry any direct evidence of material quality, the completed design drawings will always identify or imply materials. The only way to experience material quality sensorily is by having the materials themselves. Producers or processors will supply material samples, usually free of charge. Experience is thus gradually accumulated, along with a collection of materials.

🗎

\\Hint:
Trying out both the strategies for determining material quality is recommended. In this way, designers will find their own approach somewhere in the bandwidth from initial basic material-related ideas to abstract ideas that emerge without any particular material in mind. This does not imply an inflexible statement about design: the appropriate strategy always depends on the brief as well.

materials as well. Site-specific conditions such as climate and weather are crucial, as well as materials that occur naturally in the immediate vicinity. The brief also provides a framework: the function of the building and its importance, the spatial programme, and the funds available for building and running it.

Existing
buildings

The brief will often stipulate that an existing building or buildings be included or replanned; their structure, construction and material properties are then the starting-point for any subsequent decisions about design and materials. There are other general conditions that planners have to consider as well: traffic, the users' requirements, planning and building law, or specific technical requirements. The demands made on the design, the material and the structural elements derive from the sum of these conditions. The architect's task is now to explore the properties and limitations of each material selected and to translate them into a coherent construction.

For example, a site or a brief could suggest building in wood. If this organic material is exposed to moisture, this can encourage the growth of fungi and bacteria, which will damage the wood. › see chapter Wood To be used outside, it will have to be protected from the weather. For the design, this means detaching the timber structure from the ground, i.e. raised or placed on a solid base. › Fig. 68 Then the building and fire protection regulations applying to wood have to be observed: as a combustible material, it cannot be used in escape areas. If fireproof cladding is undesirable, or sprinkler facilities cannot be built on the grounds of expense, in an extreme case using wood may be out of the question.

Changeable
general
conditions

Many specific requirements are subject to change, and are not always free of contradictions. On the one hand, safety considerations continue to increase, as in fire protection, and so does ecological awareness. Users demand more and more comfort; more durable materials are sought after, as are less need for maintenance and more air conditioning. On the other, building materials no longer have to be sourced locally, as transport is easy; local identities are fading away, a random quality is creeping into the choice of materials: "anything goes" … › see chapter Material requirements

Designers have to weigh up the various general conditions carefully. They must develop a sense of how technical developments and social requirements could change building in the future. But new and innovative materials, construction methods and technologies can be set against the increasing need to reduce everything to the important and familiar in this increasingly unmanageable media society; and this make things easier to handle. These two opposite poles can show the way as helpful "guardrails" against which designers can measure their work as they move towards a position of their own and wish to test its appropriateness. This helps to formulate architecture precisely, in a way that is both close to reality and oriented towards the future.

Fig.68:
Stone column base (Japanese timber structure)

Fig.69:
Local context expressed by timber

BASING DESIGN ON MATERIAL

Tradition and
location

In historical buildings, the choice of material was usually based on what occurred naturally in the immediate vicinity of the building site; this determined whether the design could be realized or not. Local building traditions thus developed with close links to native materials. Local availability and long experience with the few materials available shaped the approach. Today, transport distances do not seem to be important at all, but regional building methods often continue to be very important, as they convey links with the locality and the region and fit in with the surroundings: think of a wooden house in a wooded area, a stone house in a rocky landscape, a brick building in a clayey region. › Fig. 69

Material
innovation

An unusual or completely new material can, however, also be the starting-point for a design. This approach is never simple, because the general conditions have to be blanked out completely at first, e.g. the typical use of a particular material or the common urban development approach to the context in question. Appropriately careful consideration should also be given to when and how the material's use is viable. For example, it might be possible to achieve new levels of comfort or durability, surface quality or cost saving with a material that is new or not customarily used in the building sector. A material that is initially unusual, used surprisingly, can be particularly expressive, and create a special atmosphere that could not be achieved by the more common one. › Fig. 70 It is still possible to address links with the locality in this way. It is precisely when classical form and innovative materials come together that architectural moods and pictures

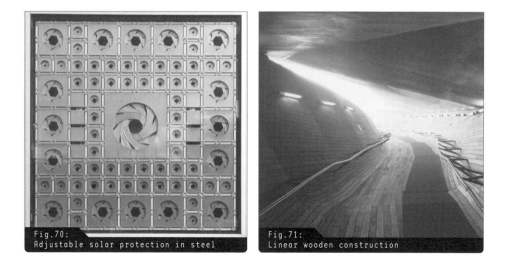

Fig.70:
Adjustable solar protection in steel

Fig.71:
Linear wooden construction

are created so that a building's materials make it shine. Thus, the simplest saddleback roof volumes, realized in an unusual way with gleaming metal surfaces or clad in coloured panels, can convey this charming aspect of the unknown and ultimately still be expressive. › Fig. 62

MATERIALIZING THE DESIGN

Materialization   As has already been mentioned, the design can also be developed independently of the material. The way materials are deployed subsequently plays a subordinate role. The designer first of all devises forms, spatial connections and links between inside and outside. The space is developed in terms of perceptual ideas; the areas creating the spaces and their effects are the prime consideration. The planner then chooses materials that will support the design's impact on this basis alone. Endowing the design with material quality issues a challenge to cross a threshold, to make the ideas more precise and concrete. Intentions are concretized by defining materials. › Fig. 72 Things acquire a presence, gradually take up the correct position in the building, and adopt the right shape. Material bestows meaning, and the visual impression, smell, tactile properties and acoustics become concrete.

Dialogue of design and material   The designer explores the materials' inherent properties. The internal forces relating to loadbearing and holding in place start to show, the principles of jointing, and ultimately also the work enshrined in things. Construction principles, component sizes and the nature of the material help to strengthen the inner logic of the design. But design, a constant interplay of emotion and intellect, only seems for a while to incline towards

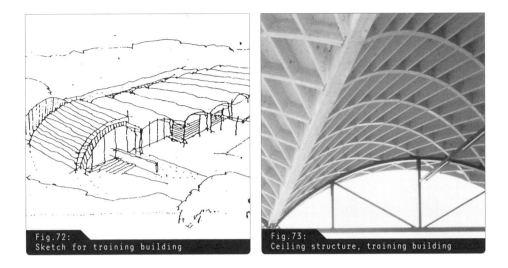

Fig.72:
Sketch for training building

Fig.73:
Ceiling structure, training building

the rational side. Using the choice of materials to comprehend and order the design can generate new emotions and ideas and offers major opportunities to improve its quality. It is helpful to check that the design as drafted is compatible with the properties of particular materials. For example, long, linear designs are well suited to directional or fibrous materials, while massive volumes suggest mineral materials. › see chapter Typologies of building materials, and Fig. 71 A loadbearing structure, for example, develops from the structure of the design, the chosen materials determine the look of the surfaces, and thus achieve the desired effect by the way they work together.

Optimization

It is advantageous if the design responds to the chosen materials, changes to accommodate the limitations imposed by their properties, and thus gains quality and character. The design formulates demands on the structure, and identifies any restrictions in the choice of materials. For example, sections of the building that form the exterior limits of interior spaces have to meet heavy demands: they must be weatherproof, windproof and ensure that interior temperatures are comfortable. Loadbearing sections must be stable and dissipate any forces acting on them without causing damage. This and other demands (such as cost) limit the range of materials that can ultimately be used to implement the idea behind the design. This kind of approach to materials gives the design an inner logic.
› Fig. 73

Transformation

Another possibility is to use the design to develop the materials. It is increasingly possible to adjust a material's properties, and in future it is conceivable that they could be tailor-made. The creativity of architects, working with the specialist knowledge of engineers and manufacturers, can push forward the development of new, highly efficient materials. This can enrich the design repertoire and improve the quality of building; or if the issues are not properly thought through, can lead to random choices and conceal technical risks.

DESIGN APPROACHES

Regardless of the design strategy chosen, decisions about materials, about their precise and meaningful use, make a crucial difference to the quality of a design and ultimately of the building that emerges. In the context of architecture, buildings can take on particular properties that are not necessarily inherent in them. They can also convey ideas that go beyond the design, and with them acquire a new sense of significance. Materials are central elements in the language of architecture. Their vocabulary demonstrates some sets of rules that apply particularly to material quality, which will be examined in more detail below.

Monolith (sculptural effect, physical presence)

Monolithic building

Monolithic building is a material-dependent design principle. Often only a limited range of materials was available locally, and sometimes only a single material could be used for all building needs. The Egyptian pyramids, the Pantheon in Rome and medieval castles appear, and are, monolithic. › Fig. 74

If a single material is used, it dominates the statement the architecture makes. In modern architecture, fair-face concrete buildings seem to interpret the term "monolith" almost literally: the building looks as though it is made "of one stone", here artificial stone. › see chapter Concrete A monolithic impression can also be conveyed by other material, such as brick, › see chapter Ceramics and bricks and so can natural stone used as a curtain wall, erected homogeneously with discreet joints. › see chapter Natural stone The aim is always to create a completely homogeneous spatial effect. Architecture always tries to create a meaningful whole, and a monolithic approach to

\\Tip:
Giving material quality to a design means first studying materials intensively. It is worth familiarizing oneself with the variety of materials on offer in the building industry, and with specimen products. Examining both customary and unusual material applications and analysing their technical and sensory properties gradually leads to formulating an individual position, which is the basis for independent approaches and ideas.

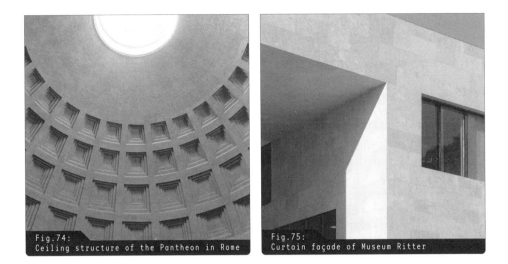

Fig.74:
Ceiling structure of the Pantheon in Rome

Fig.75:
Curtain façade of Museum Ritter

design means this happens almost automatically. The surfaces and the internal structure are made of one and the same material – or at least that is how it seems. Because if it really were just one material, it would have to meet as many of the demands as possible the building itself is intended to meet.

This ideal is becoming increasingly difficult to realize as more and more demands are made on our buildings. Solid walls in natural stone, for example, could no longer match today's comfort requirements, and would also hardly be affordable. So the surface and the internal structure are often no longer identical, but usually consist of different components. › see chapter Concrete The outer, fair-face concrete façade conceals the thermal insulation, pipework and wires, and many other things. Each element has its own defined part to play, and is particularly suited to it, e.g. supporting, reinforcing, insulating or sealing. Even large areas of natural stone cladding,

\\ Tip:
The effect of a monolithic building approach, and thus of architecture with considerable physical presence, is created by a subtractive design. This implies the sparing use of apertures cut deep into the body of the structure, or wide apertures that become part of the monolithic surface, if they are made completely flush with the surface, with slender frames, and if the reflecting surfaces correspond with similar surfaces in the opaque body of the building.

bricks, plaster and – in the interior – plasterboard can look monolithic if the joints are designed to be very discreet or seamless. The finish on the edges of the building is then particularly important if the monolithic impression is to be maintained. If there were evidence here of how thin the cladding actually is, or even of open joints, the solid appearance of the building would be jeopardized. Cornerstones and closed joints reinforce the monolithic effect. > Fig. 75

Layers and surfaces

Function

If technical demands are to be met as fully as possible, areas made up of various layers are almost unavoidable. This does not apply to outer walls alone, but also to roofs, ceilings, and even interior walls with heavy demands made on them. Load dissipation and reinforcement, insulation and sealing, sound- and fireproofing, moisture regulation and damage prevention – these are just some of the demands that a sequence of layers has to meet. > see chapter Material requirements, Maintaining function

Visible / invisible layers

This layering cannot be seen within transparent areas. In normal double or triple glazing, the panes of glass are responsible for sealing, and provide insulating gaps, with inert gas injected to improve their heat and sound insulation effects. Coatings reflect heat back into the room or offer protection from undue exposure to sunlight. > see chapter Glass Developing a sequence of layers meaningfully from the functional demands on each component layer is one of the architect's key tasks. The requirements each component has to meet should be listed and assigned to different areas. Individual materials are then chosen on the basis of their technical properties to meet these requirements, and the parts then become functional layers within a whole. > see chapter Technical properties The different layers have different useful lives, which must relate to each other correctly, just like the technical and design characteristics.

Surface area design

As the various layers are assembled by area, it is not the body of the building as a whole (as in the monolithic approach), but the individual area that is the key visual feature. Likewise, the way these areas are fitted together evokes different images: division rather than cohesion, lightness to the point of fragility, movement rather than statuesque repose. > Fig. 76

These areas do not have to end at the edges of the building to make a visual impact; they can end before them, or protrude beyond them, so that their effect as surface areas is clearly visible. The layers can dissolve at their edges, become diffuse. Or parts of the structure can be removed to reveal parts of the layer structure, thereby increasing understanding of their structure, the building process and thus of the building as a whole. > Fig. 77

A surface area design reaches its theoretical peak in surface areas that are as thin as possible and look two-dimensional. On the other hand,

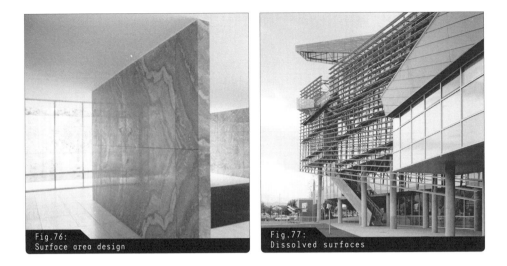

Fig.76:
Surface area design

Fig.77:
Dissolved surfaces

the technical demand is for greater thickness of material, especially of insulating layers. The impression of slender surface quality is emphasized by revealing layers and by visually detaching cladding from its substructure. Metallic cladding in particular, › see chapter Metals but also glass or plastics, › see chapters Glass, Plastics make such effects possible because they can be produced in very thin finishes.

Unity and diversity

From
homogeneous to
heterogeneous

It is not only the different layers of a building that are based on different materials, with each one playing its particular part. The surface of any building can also be subject to demands that are not uniform, or may even be contradictory, and cannot be met by a single material. The materials chosen for the individual parts and functions then reflect these differences: for example, the base of the building is subject to mechanical loads, and has to cope with moisture, and so is different from the rising walls and their coverings; the front and back of a building should also create different effects. Functions within a building can also be illustrated by the nature of the materials chosen. The variety of materials can affect the scale and proportion of a building, and create images for façades and spaces that could not be achieved by using the same material homogeneously throughout. › see chapter Perception of materials, Visual This can become a kind of collage, in which a whole variety of ordinary materials (possibly including scrap materials) can be placed in a new and unusual context and convey a lack of completeness, while shedding new light on elements that are not much esteemed. › Fig. 78

Fig.78:
Collage of materials

Fig.79:
Transparency and lightness

Tension arising
from diversity
Playing with the wide range of materials available offers new opportunities, but it also implies technical structural risks arising from different properties of materials that are suddenly juxtaposed. If this field of tension arising from a variety of materials produces architecture, the qualities of that architecture will not derive from the significance of an established material, but will make the variety itself the key feature. The complexity of the materials is thereby recognized, and expresses itself in heterogeneous structures. The contrast between the different materials leads to new connections and tensions. Different surfaces, colours and sensory effects quite deliberately convey a difference in meaning and create different moods. › Fig. 78

Structure and surfaces

Loadbearing
structure and
surface
Architecture has to acknowledge gravity, but does not have to demonstrate it. So there are two possible and contrasting approaches to handling the loadbearing structure: the design can illustrate the structure and its supporting function, or deliberately conceal it, to the point of apparently defying gravity. As has been shown, a cubic or even a monolithic approach underlines the essence of the structure. But dissolving the volumes into separate areas makes an effect of lightness, and shifts the structure into the background. The nature of the materials makes a key contribution to creating a sense of lightness or heaviness, initially through the placing, dimensions and design of the loadbearing elements. Particularly efficient materials such as steel, make small structural cross sections possible. Smooth surfaces enhance the impression of lightness. › Fig. 79

Colours or patterns extending over an extensive surface area can take the effect of lightness to the point of apparent dissolution. Fine renderings, panels and shiny surfaces, in glazed tiles, for example, are particularly appropriate here. The textures of highly polished natural stone and glass can form skin that seems continuous, apparently no longer disadvantaged by necessary apertures. › Fig. 77

Surfaces of this kind shimmer and change constantly as the viewer moves. Surfaces can look like light, transparent wraps if they use expanded metal, wire mesh or perforated metal panels. › see chapter Metals Closed surfaces with fine reliefs in plaster or natural stone can make a similar effect. At the other end of the scale is rough, rusticated ashlar, the epitome of solidity and weight. Brick walls make a similar effect so long as the bricks are rough in texture and matte. The choice of masonry bond, especially in terms of jointing and mortar, makes a key contribution to the overall impression.
› see chapter Ceramics and bricks

Very small differences can influence the appearance of a building considerably: smooth or textured, rough or decorative, with joints or a plane surface, even or finely flecked. These differences can be inherent in the material itself. For example, natural stone in a homogeneous colour in relation to a finely veined one, or one with lively flaming; the diversity of brick colours from yellowish brown via glowing red to reddish brown; or the almost infinite range of different types of wood. Subtle differences are also created by the way materials are processed. › see chapter Classification of materials Material coatings add another dimension: colourless or coloured, flat or glazed.

Joints and connections

At first glance, joints and connections are secondary elements that combine parts to form a whole. They necessarily occur where parts of the building that are different or the same come together, or they separate parts of a building or façade, to give them a different sense of movement or placement. But essentially they feature as elements that remain visible.

But essentially a joint as a separating element demonstrates not the separation of materials, but their composition. They are parts of the build-

✎

\\ Tip:
When developing the patterns made by joints the first sources of guidance are the methods that are typically used, simply and obviously, for joining and connecting a material. They can make a design look lucid and logical. Then other, freer developments are possible on this basis: for example, an abstract pattern of joints can make the design look more dynamic.

ing that are not made of a particular material, but do derive from its properties. Joints illustrate the elements of a material, whether it is the material itself or its negative form, as cladding. Joints create patterns, fixing the detail of intermediate stages within the larger proportions of a building. These joint patterns are based on technical requirements such as the format sizes of materials available, the spacing of expansion joints, or the nature of a particular part of the building. But the designer is always free to create a pattern of joints in keeping with the creative ideas involved: this can develop logically from the demands made by the articulation of the storeys, the loadbearing structure, and the arrangement of the apertures. He or she can also deliberately conceal these factors and overlay them with independent patterns. › Fig. 79 Ultimately, the pattern of joints makes a major contribution to the formal rhythm of the building and the finer aspects of its scale. In masonry, closed mortar jointing, for example, creates a massive impression and makes the design look homogeneous and heavy. Raked-out brick joints reinforce the image of the horizontally layered wall. In the case of thin cladding, however, open joints can reveal the structure behind them, showing that the material used is a layer. › Fig. 80

Fastenings   Connections can be visible or invisible, as in natural stone curtain walls, or the screws used to fix wood-based panels. Their first task is to ensure that components are positioned precisely, but they must also accommodate the material's movement: this is minimal in the case of stone, but is a crucial factor for wood and metal. Invisible fastenings underline the uniform quality of a material. Visible screws signal precision workmanship, as well as simplicity and the possibility of change. If fastenings are repeated in a particular rhythm they can make a considerable difference to the appearance of a building. Rivets on a steel structure demonstrate the flow of forces. › Fig. 81 Like many other visible connections, they convey an impression of the jointing and connecting process in architecture.

Effect of joints   Joints and connections can emphasize the nature of a material and thus contribute to a coherent overall image. But they can also conceal features deliberately, which can make an even greater impact than the material. Then the joint pattern or the connecting element dominates the design with an independent expressive quality of its own, pushing the material into the background. Ultimately, joints and connections are there to serve the overall idea, and to enhance its presence. They have to be addressed, because a building consists of countless parts. These parts, all with different functions, materials, shapes and sizes, should ultimately form a whole. The nature of their final form decides whether the details of a building convey coherence or separation, tension or lightness, strength or fragility.

Fig.80:
Jointing as a performance

Fig.81:
Hauptbahnhof, Frankfurt

IN CONCLUSION

The choice, processing and detailing of material play key parts in the design process. Form and material should blend to create a consistent unity.

Material quality

The purely visual level, conveyed by optical perception of a material, usually comes first: colour, texture, reflective qualities, jointing and many other aspects. Perception via the other senses is closely linked: how the material feels when touched, its smell, its acoustic and thermal properties. The internal properties of a material, such as physical structure, loadbearing capacity, durability and the many ways in which materials affect the environment, are largely invisible. These objective "inner values" define what is technically feasible and make the ultimate material realization logical and meaningful. Ultimately, every material is defined by the meaning it conveys. Many people agree about such value judgements, but they cannot be analysed objectively; and so they can be reinterpreted and endowed with surprising new levels of significance.

Materialization

Giving material form to a design is an extremely exciting process, which combines sensory experience, specialist knowledge, and usually a delight in experimentation as well. It is only in the creative process, when possible ways of alienating materials are tried out, and the material is considered in a wide range of new forms and structures, that harmony can be achieved between design and material quality, and brief, form and material can be made to work together happily. Drawings, models and material tests can make something that has not yet been built look as though it already exists – even though it is not really there yet.

APPENDIX

LITERATURE

Borch, Keuning, Kruit, Melet, Peterse, Vollaard, de Vries, Zijlstra: *Skins for Buildings*, BIS Publishers, Amsterdam 2004

Deplazes (ed.): *Constructing Architecture*, Birkhäuser Publishers, Basel 2005

Hegger, Auch-Schwelk, Fuchs, Rosenkranz: *Construction Materials Manual*, Birkhäuser Publishers, Basel 2005

Hugues, Steiger, Weber: *Detail Practice: Dressed Stone*, Birkhäuser Publishers, Basel 2005

Kaltenbach (ed.): Detail Practice: *Translucent Materials*, Birkhäuser Publishers, Basel 2004

Koch: *Membrane Structures*, Prestel Publishing, Munich 2004

Reichel, Hochberg, Köpke: *Detail Practice: Plaster, Render, Paint and Coating*, Birkhäuser Publishers, Basel 2005

Wilhide: *Materials*, Quadrille Publishing, London 2003

Magazines

DETAIL Magazine for Architecture, Materials + Surfaces, 6/2006, Institut für internationale Architekturdokumentation, Munich 2006

PICTURE CREDITS

ALSO AVAILABLE FROM BIRKHÄUSER:

Basics Design and Living
Jan Krebs
ISBN 3-7643-7647-3

Basics Modelbuilding
Alexander Schilling
ISBN 3-7643-7649-X

Basics Technical Drawing
Bert Bielefeld, Isabella Skiba
ISBN 3-7643-7644-9

Basics Masonry Construction
Nils Kummer
ISBN 3-7643-7645-7

Basics Roof Construction
Tanja Brotrück
ISBN 3-7643-7683-X

Series editor: Bert Bielefeld
Conception: Bert Bielefeld, Annette Gref
Layout and Cover design: Muriel Comby
Text and picture setting: Viola John
Picture editor: Sebastian Sprenger
Translation into English: Michael Robinson
English Copy editing: Monica Buckland

A CIP catalogue record for this book is available
from the Library of Congress, Washington D.C.,
USA

Bibliographic information published by
Die Deutsche Bibliothek
Die Deutsche Bibliothek lists this publication
in the Deutsche Nationalbibliografie; detailed
bibliographic data is available on the Internet at
http://dnb.ddb.de.

This book is also available in a German
(ISBN 3-7643-7684-8) and a French
(ISBN 3-7643-7954-5) language edition.

© 2007 Birkhäuser –Publishers for Architecture,
P.O. Box 133, CH-4010 Basel, Switzerland
Member of Springer Science + Business Media

Printed on acid-free paper produced from
chlorine-free pulp. TCF ∞
Printed in Germany

ISBN-10: 3-7643-7685-6
ISBN-13: 978-3-7643-7685-7

9 8 7 6 5 4 3 2 1   www.birkhauser.ch